GEOFFREY

Printed in Great Britain by
WHITEHEAD & MILLER LTD.
ELMWOOD LANE
LEEDS 7

GEOFFREY

Major JOHN GEOFFREY APPLEYARD

D.S.O., M.C. and BAR, M.A.

BEING THE STORY OF
"A P P L E"
OF
THE COMMANDOS
AND
SPECIAL AIR SERVICE REGIMENT

BY J.E.A.

1946
BLANDFORD PRESS LTD.
16 WEST CENTRAL STREET
LONDON, W.C.1

This book was first written for Geoffrey's friends and is dedicated to his memory.

After many requests, the book has now been given wider publication, in the hope that it may help to perpetuate the Commando spirit of adventure and selfless endeavour and sacrifice amongst the rising generation in days of peace.

All royalties arising from the sale of this book will be divided equally between The Commandos' Benevolent Fund and The Special Air Service Regimental Association.

Preface

In the selected letters Geoffrey painted his own ·portrait—unwittingly, for he never dreamt of publication. With the help of his comrades-in-arms and the family I have provided only the canvas. The letters are left in their original form, though omitting many endearing greetings, cheery endings and loving references to the letters received by him from home.

Geoffrey only lived to be twenty-six, but the quality and value of a life cannot be measured by its length.

As Philip James Bailey says :—

We live in deeds, not years ; in thoughts, not breaths ;
In feelings, not in figures on a dial.
We should count time by heart-throbs. He most lives
Who thinks most—feels the noblest—acts the best.

J.E.A.
(Geoffrey's father.)

A Trinity of Arms

PRAYER FOR COMBINED OPERATIONS

O LORD GOD, our Father, our Saviour, our Might, we pray Thee take into Thy keeping us who are joined together in a trinity of arms on sea, on land, and in the air in this our special service for King and Country.

We pledge ourselves to do, to dare, to die that others may live, believing in Him who said : " Greater love hath no man than this, that a man lay down his life for his friends."

Grant us faith, courage, and determination that we fail not in whatever duty may lie before us, and may we be enabled by Thy Divine Grace to bear our part in establishing peace on earth and goodwill amongst men.

This we ask for Jesus Christ, His sake.

Amen.

Contents

Illustrations

The author gratefully thanks the writers of letters which are quoted, and the photographers whose pictures are reproduced, for the privilege of using them in this book.

GEOFFREY

CHAPTER I

SCHOOL AND COLLEGE DAYS

GEOFFREY WAS BORN in Bramley, Leeds, on December 20th, 1916, in the middle of the war that was to end wars. In 1921, his family celebrated his fifth birthday by moving to the Manor House, Linton-on-Wharfe, near Wetherby, Yorkshire. There, in the old house and garden and in the midget rowing boat on the pool he spent the happiest of childhoods with his two sisters and younger brother. This early experience of " combined operations " by land and water was no small part of their enjoyment. After a small local school he attended Moorlands School, Headingley, and in 1931 moved to Bootham, York, a school of the Society of Friends, for his serious education but, being Geoff, one fears he did not take it very seriously. His gay, light-hearted adventurous spirit soon asserted itself and he was far more interested in planning and executing his wide-flung ornithological expeditions, or organising a midnight rag, otherwise known at Bootham as a " rabble," than in really studious work. He became Secretary of the Natural History Society and devoted much time to originating and developing the school's activities in conjunction with the British Museum in the " ringing " or " banding " of birds, with a view to investigating the laws of migration, and many interesting " recoveries " of these Bootham rings proved the movement of British birds to and from South Africa, Algiers, Russia, Norway, Denmark and even Greenland. For these original activities he was awarded the school's coveted " Natural History Exhibition."

The possibilities of the school walls and roof were irresistible attractions to his climbing propensities. One morning the master on duty called him to his study.

A

" You were on the roof last night, Geoffrey ! " " Yes, sir, but how did you know ? " " I saw your silhouette, you silly wet," was the reply. The incident was a lesson in camouflage to be applied in more serious raids in graver times.

Another night, Geoff and his co-ringleaders decided on a towards-the-end-of-term rabble and supper in the bedroom. Travelling trunks were piled high upon each other in irremovable jams at the strategic corners of the approaching corridors and the supper proceeded in security until the sound of revelry by night attracted masters and rival " Reeves " from other Houses and the assault and defence of the barricades began—another gay pre-view of graver things to follow.

For long, and as a triumphant exhibit to later school-boy generations, there remained on the wall of one of the bedrooms of Bootham a picture frame containing the proud trophy of a piece of Geoffrey's pyjamas secured in repelling a midnight raid led by him from a rival bedroom.

How great is one's admiration of the broadness of mind and generosity of judgment of the Bootham masters when, with such provocation, Donald Gray, the Head, could report on 31/3/32 "A boy of very attractive character who causes a great deal of trouble by thoughtless high spirits. He takes punishment in the right spirit but generally contrives to ' do it again ' very soon. Good manners, healthy and friendly." His House master, Leslie Gilbert, added " I admire his absolute straightforwardness ; it seems to be the pattern on which he builds his life. It is difficult to praise enough his sincere, friendly attitude in all things, even in his occasional outbreaks of harmless disorder." By March, 1934, the report was a little better: "A very good term all round, though his work is sometimes neglected for his hobbies. A thoroughly good influence in the school." By April, 1935, the lure of Cambridge and the necessity of passing the Entrance Examination were making themselves felt, and it was a relief to read in that term's report "A very good term, conscientious, sensible and hardworking on the whole. A very good companion, excellent manners, and a good representative of the school."

This concentration, of which he was always capable when convinced it was necessary, bore its reward in successful examinations and he was admitted to Caius College, Cambridge, for the term commencing October 1935.

Geoff found delight in Cambridge. Not, one fears, in much hard work until towards the end, but in ceaseless activity principally in rowing during term, qualifying as a member of the College Eight, becoming College Boat Club Secretary in his second year and " Captain of the Boats " in his final year, very nearly a full-time job. A typical disciplinary notice reveals " the iron hand in the velvet glove " :—

C.B.C., Saturday, November 6th.

All boats will go into training for the Fairbairn Cup Races after midnight to-night. The following rules must be observed :—

No smoking at all.

No alcoholic drinks except beer. Drink as little of this as possible, preferably only in Hall at night, and don't drink for the sake of drinking. Never more than two pints a day.

In bed by 10-30 *p.m.*—don't stay late in bed in the mornings.

No eating between meals.

Don't have baths too hot or too long. Five minutes is plenty.

Cultivate regular " habits " !

J. G. APPLEYARD
(Capt. C.B.C.)

But this strictness is tempered by his notes on the coaching of an Eight. " Persuasion and encouragement can do more to ' bring a crew on ' than abuse and scorn—I have felt that myself when being coached by the latter type and so know which has the best moral effect (and therefore physical effect) on one's rowing and attitude to the sport in general. Discouragement only makes one fed up and stubborn ! "

The culmination of the rowing season in the May's Races of '37 and '38 and the Royal Regattas at Henley, following weeks of Spartan training ; the exertion in the races to the very limit of endurance with every man of the eight trained to give all he had up to the point of collapse at the winning post—such team work and endeavour were to Geoffrey at that time amongst the really great and important things in life. Rowing gave him rippling muscles and superb physique.

Happy long June nights followed the May's Week in a round of college balls lasting all night long, ending with breakfast down the river.

But it was in ski-ing rather than rowing that he made his mark as a sportsman. His first tour with the University Team was to Breuil in Italy, under the Matterhorn, in December 1936.

This is his description of his first morning there : " Woke this morning to a perfect Swiss morning, cold with perfect blue sky and the sun shining, the trees piled up with snow and weighed down under it. I walked out on to the terrace—and positively gasped ! There was the Matterhorn right away up in the sky— towering above the village and sparkling white with powder snow wherever snow could find a resting place on its terrific crags, and then to the left of the Matter- horn, pinnacles and spires of rock and crag all gleaming in the bright sunshine and so dazzling that I was momentarily blinded after the dark hotel and had to shut my eyes ! It was tremendous—on every side mountains towering right up and up and up, with here and there wisps of cloud and all covered with a flashing white mantle of snow ! One really feels to be amongst the high mountains here—they go sheer up out of the valley on every side and one's first thought is

' Dolomites ' ! The Cervino (Matterhorn) fills up the end of the valley—it looks majestic from this side—not so precipitous and spire-like as from the Zermatt side, but stronger and more solid, like Monte Cristalo as seen from the road between Misurina and Cortina."

At Breuil, Oxford and Cambridge men were coached by Gasperl, the holder of the Kilometre Lancé World's Record at St. Moritz and an Olympic skier, and great was the competition to be chosen for Cambridge in the Inter-Varsity Race and so win the coveted " Ski-ing Blue." Says Geoff, who was learning a lesson he soon applied in other ways of life, " I'm afraid my chances of getting into the team are very remote. When I'm really fast I'm not in control, and when I'm in control I'm not fast enough to keep up with the cracks who are both fast and controlled—but I'm going to keep on trying for the team—there might be a sudden improvement." But he did not get a place that first year.

Not all the ski-ing was by daylight, as the following extract records. " Last night's torchlight ski-ing party was really enormous fun ! About forty people from the two clubs went up in the bucket, and in the hut at the top we were received by the Cervinia Ski Club who welcomed the clubs to Cervinia—there were various speeches, etc.—songs, we all ' saluta Duce'd ' in the approved style and had a supper—altogether a very jolly and rowdy international party ! Only ten of us skied down at 11 p.m.—the rest preferred to return by funicular as it was snowing slightly. Most of both teams skied down, also myself and one or two others, and it was terrific sport ! It was a pitch dark night— not a star in the sky—but we were provided with torches —one each—which we held in the same hand as one ski-stick—and really these gave a remarkably good light. The snow was in perfect condition and somehow I was third down and had a no-fall run. It was most amusing to look back after running a bit and see these lights darting about all over the hillside at what appeared in the dark incredible speeds and then a light would come rushing towards you and suddenly waver and

6 GEOFFREY

abruptly go out as the bearer buried it in the snow on falling ! The air was full of shouts and muffled cursings and laughter above all—it was a riotous affair ! The lights gave a view ahead of about 15 feet and were of the usual torch variety—candle-wax and paraffin (?) round a wick. They burnt well. The wall jump was especially thrilling. You know you can't see the ground beyond the wall at all until you are in the air and it may be strewn with bodies for all the warning one has, as, on falling, the lights invariably went out. This created quite a lot of excitement ! "

On the day before Christmas, from Breuil with a companion he accomplished the feat of climbing the mountain frontier range near the Breithorn, ski-ing down the glacier to Zermatt in Switzerland, and climbing back in moonlight over the Theodul Pass and down to Italy—considered an impossible run for one day. That was typically Geoffrey—always trying to surpass the accepted limit of endurance. The guides would not go—they said it could not be done in one day.

The following winter in 1937 found the Cambridge skiers at Davos in Switzerland and training under Willi Walch, the Austrian Champion, and a big crowd of men in the running for selection in the team and the consequent award of the coveted " Blue." The *Daily Mail* spoke of the hundreds of university men hurling themselves down at incredible speed from the Weissfluhjoch and the many broken legs and collar bones, and advised those who think young Englishmen decadent to come out and see for themselves. Just before Christmas, an ecstatic letter arrived home from Geoff : " Hurrah !—made it—the team for the Inter-Varsity Downhill and Slalom was announced half an hour ago—whoopee ! ! and so one of my greatest ambitions has been realised and I have got my ' Blue ' at Cambridge." The race was run on December 20th, his twenty-first birthday. " The Downhill race against Oxford is due to begin from the Men's Tee at 11 a.m. and so I must pass an anxious hour before going up on the 10 train, to allow half an hour at the top to enable one to get used to the height and thus be stronger in the legs on the first *schuss*. My skis are waxed until they reflect and every quarter of an hour I tighten my boots up so that by 11 o'clock they are as solid on the feet as blocks of concrete. The day has dawned sunny and cloudless and is a perfect day for a downhill race— thank goodness, because yesterday there was a tremendous cloud down over the tops and visibility was only a very few feet right down to the 'Alpine Gardens.' It really was epic to wake up this morning and feel that such a great day was at hand—my 21st birthday and the races for Cambridge against Oxford! It really is thrilling that they should coincide like this and it couldn't have been arranged better." And no present could have been so sweet as the one that fell to his lot for that very day he won the Slalom Race for Cambridge against the rival Oxford Team.

To commemorate the race and his " twenty-first," the Cambridge team presented Geoff with a beautifully designed silver cigarette box surmounted by the figure of a skier in racing posture. It was inscribed with the University coat of arms and the signatures of the Cambridge men. Alas! the majority of that gallant band have " finished the course " for their country in a greater race.

Geoff also came in second in the Langlauf eighteen-mile cross-country race against Oxford, and was one of the first University pair in the roped ski race against Davos. Of this he wrote : " There are few things more exciting than when roped stoutly to another man you find yourselves likely to be on different sides of a strong 10-foot post and travelling at forty miles per hour." A week later at Zermatt he was first in the open race of the Monte Rosa Robinson open challenge cup and one of the winning three in the inter-hotel relay ski race.

Geoff as a skier had now arrived.

He accepted an invitation to captain an English Team to ski against Norway in the Easter vacation of 1938 and by way of training developed the novel idea of grass ski-ing on the steep slopes of Dunstable Downs. The new sport was pioneered by Geoff and three other ski blues who at once were nicknamed " The Grasshoppers." The press, illustrated papers and news films made much of the new summer and winter ski-ing, referring to Cambridge University as " an ever-progressing centre of learning."

The opening match of the tour against the West Coast of Norway went very well. The visitors beat the Norwegians on their own ground, at Myrdal, and their papers were frankly astonished. Geoffrey was first in the Downhill, fifth in the Slalom and gained the highest aggregate of marks on them both to win the event for England and become Anglo-Norwegian Champion 1938. Here is his own account :—

" Yesterday was the Downhill. The course is absolutely incredible—steep as a house side and the fastest thing on earth. The start was at one o'clock and was in a howling wind which blew up the snow and the sky was overcast and cloudy, making seeing very difficult and necessitating visors and goggles, etc. In fact, conditions were about as bad as they could be. It was terribly cold and miserable waiting at the top for the start and I started last but one ! (That is, last of the English.)

" The forerunner was Carl Christian—a magnificent runner and known as the wildest skier in Norway. This time his wildness was successful and he returned the amazing time of 1 minute 12 seconds for the 2 Km. descent of exactly 2,000 feet ! He went off in a lull of the storm and so was not held back by the wind as were all the competitors in the race. Still it was an incredible performance. I went off in a particularly vile piece of head wind, but I certainly had the race of my life and have never enjoyed anything so much before. The incredible closeness of the race is shown by the fact that the first seven competitors were all under 5 seconds of the first man and that I was only 6/10ths of a second faster than Garrow who got second place.   Muir coming fourth made it look as though our chance of the team event was pretty good and there was terrific excitement waiting for $1\frac{1}{2}$ hours whilst the complicated mathematics, which determined each man's score in the Combined, was being worked out, and of course we were enormously thrilled when we were told that the English team were the winners by 577.4 to 587.9—about as close as it could be.   I was amazed at winning the Combined and thus being the Anglo-Norwegian Champion 1938, as I thought my Slalom had been too steady.   Note again the closeness of the first five in the Combined—especially numbers 2, 3 and 4, all being within 3/10ths of a second ! !

" The Norwegians are all absolutely delighted that we have won—far more pleased than if their own team had won—it's amazing !   As you know this is only the second year of the Anglo-Norwegian contest, and last year all three trophies—Downhill, Slalom and Combined—were won by Per Fossum, the Norwegian Olympic, and so my name will go on the Downhill and Combined cups underneath his, which is rather cheek I feel !   They are two lovely cups and I have been given a little replica for keeps of each of them.   In addition to this, we shall bring back across the sea the Anglo-Norwegian team trophy which last year remained in Norway, and which as Captain of the English team, it will be my proud duty to look after for the next year. It's a great thing about 12″ high, and so make way for it in the lounge !   It is a lovely cup.

" There has been a news-reel photographer here for this event and he has taken 150 metres (500 feet) of film of the races which is to be shown in all the cinemas in Norway and also, so he says, in England."

It so happened that this race coincided with the 'Varsity Boat Race in London when Oxford decisively beat the Light Blues.   On receipt of the Ski Race result, Geoff's sister Margot, a Somerville, Oxford girl, cabled him " Delighted—congratulations—Cambridge *can* ski, can't row."

The English team then went on tour for some days across the Jotunheim Mountains to Spiterstulen at the foot of the Galdhopiggen Mountain, the highest in Norway. Geoff had better give his own impressions.

" This is the most wonderful country that ever was—and I think the Norwegians are the finest people I have ever met—they are great guys ! We have had absolutely glorious weather—I think only one day has not been absolutely perfect—by that I mean continuous sunshine all day, with never the trace of a cloud and a deep blue sky. My face has never been so brown before—it must be almost unrecognisable. Also we've frequently been ski-ing without shirts. Jove, it's been absolutely marvellous. I'd have to write a book about it all to give you a proper impression, but I'll let you have all news in full when I get home, so here is a brief résumé.

" We left Spiterstulen with great reluctance for four days' tour across 200 miles of country southwards to Myrdal. A wonderful trip that I'll always remember. Living in huts of course. Finally arrived here on foot after using motor-boats on lakes, steamers on the fjords (a night on one), car, dog-sleds, etc.

" Must stop and eat. These boys have the right ideas about food—no continental breakfasts. Compared with breakfast here, even the Dutch equivalent is an infant's meal. Other meals also compare more than favourably with breakfast. Sheer bliss ! Time is quite neglected. You arrive and leave places at incredible hours. You eat at 10-30 a.m., 3-30 p.m., 8 p.m. Call the meals what you want. I never know if breakfast is lunch, and lunch, dinner ! Enormously fit—more than ever before. What a life ! Heaps of love, Geoff."

Geoffrey's winter sports' interests were not confined to ski-ing. He was an expert ice hockey player and was a member of the Cambridge Eskimos team. As such he was offered a place on a European tour and had to choose between this and competing in the 'Varsity Ski Races against Oxford. As already described, he elected for the sport of the snow rather than that of the ice on the grounds of greater freedom of the wide open spaces which it offered.

Geoff and his sister, Joyce, were amongst the first English men and women to learn and love ski-ing on yet another element—water, towed, to keep afloat, by a rope attached to a speed boat moving at not less than thirty knots. By request they gave exhibitions in Scarborough and Bridlington bays to astonished spectators who crowded the piers. This was thought to be the first demonstration of this sport in the north of England.

Geoffrey's bird-loving activities were continued at Cambridge. One day, great excitement was created amongst the ornithologists by the observation of a black redstart, a rare visitant to Britain and one whose nesting places in these islands, except on sea cliffs, had only rarely been recorded. He told the story in *The Granta* under the title "A Distinguished Foreign Visitor," and here is part of it :—

" Hardly daring to believe in the possibility, we decided to get to some vantage point from which we could see where the birds were flying, and the roof seemed to be the most obvious place. Although it was raining hard, we determined to waste no time, because, if young were being fed, they might be in quite an advanced stage and soon leaving the nest, after which it would be almost impossible to trace them. We took to the roofs.

" Soon we got an idea of the direction in which they were going and, barefooted to get a better grip on the slippery tiles, we moved from one roof to its neighbour, then across another, and on to the next, and so on, sometimes with their owner's permission, but usually without, for from above it is amazingly difficult to find out whose roof you are on, and frequently their owners expressed considerable surprise to find us ensconced thereon ! However, on realising the cause of our strange behaviour they entered into the spirit of the hunt and rallied round, providing ladders where essential (and advice where thought necessary) in a most generous fashion.

" Finally, after a considerable search, we saw one of the birds fly downwards to a point in the middle of a wall on one side of a backyard, wait a few seconds, and then fly away again in the direction of the feeding ground. We quickly made our way over to the spot, and heard the hunger calls of young birds coming from behind a drain-pipe, some depth down a hole in the wall which had been formed by a piece of brick falling out.

" So here was the nest of a black redstart ! And in what unexpected surroundings ! Instead of its normal home in some deep crack in a sea-cliff, here were a pair of birds nesting behind a drain-pipe, ten feet away from the window of a room in which thirty or forty girls were working at noisy machines—below, a small yard with people continually passing backwards and forwards across it, and all within a few paces of Cambridge's busy market place ! "

Geoffrey's bird ' ringing ' or ' banding ' activities were originally carried on along with two Bootham school friends, Michael Rowntree and Archie Willis, who were later assisted by Geoff's younger brother Ian, who afterwards took over the work when the war disbanded the original partnership. From the three surnames they coined the name " WIPPLETREE " and reported their activities to the British Museum under this name. One of the successful ringings was a young pied wagtail from a nest in the Linton Manor garden and the following spring found in North Africa near Algiers. British Birds, the official ornithological journal described this recovery as one of the most interesting of the year, and The Yorkshire Post attributed it to " that enthusiastic amateur who prefers to hide his anonymity under the pseudonym of ' Wippletree.' "

On one ornithological expedition, Geoff persuaded the gatherer of the gulls' eggs on the Bempton cliffs, near Flamborough, to permit him to take his place on the loop of rope and be lowered over the edge, where he swung himself to and fro, hundreds of feet above the sea, until able to make contact with the side of the overhanging cliff and gather the coveted trophy as a proof of success.

Back to Cambridge for his last term, and apparently with a determination to make up in his studies for " the years that the locust hath eaten," he passed over to others many of his rowing activities, and not only devoted himself to hard work for his own examination, but coached a friend, whose hopes of success were very slender, through the whole course, thereby, he alleged, firmly laying the foundations for himself and finding out what he didn't know by what he couldn't teach. He must have applied to work all the immense powers of concentration he had previously devoted to sport for, although not a brilliant student, he surprised all his friends, and probably himself, by achieving a First Class in the B.A. Engineering Degree. The Boat Club were scurrilous that a rowing man should pull off a First and sent amusing telegrams :—

"Appleyard, Caius. Send particulars of exam. *Daily Mirror.*"

"Appleyard, Caius. Scoop of the century, circulation shooting up. Beaverbrook."

"Appleyard, Caius. Gad, Sir, the boys are proud of their Captain. Youzah."

The Senior Tutor of Caius at the Farewell Dinner inscribed on Geoff's menu card : " I hope you are as glad to be here as I am that you came." And to Geoff's home the tutor wrote : "Academic distinctions are not everything and I think it is the merit of Cambridge to recognise the value and importance of other qualities in a young man as well. I shall always remember Geoffrey with gratitude and affection for his contribution to the life of the College and shall miss his cheery presence next year."

Geoff came down from Cambridge a happy man, with his two great ambitions fulfilled—a First in Engineering, and a Blue—it is feared he valued the latter more than the former !

Geoff had previously spent much time in the 'Varsity vacations in the motor repair depot of his father's business. He entered in earnest after the summer vacation of 1938, characteristically donning overalls and starting at the bottom, intent on learning every section of its activities at first hand. At the Christmas Annual Staff Dinner, when called upon for a speech, he replied : " Facing all of you to-night, some of whom have been with us for ten or fifteen or more years, I feel that it is rather out of place for me to be getting upon my feet at all—even for only two minutes. You see, I've always been told that children should be seen and not heard, and as I've only been working since September, I'm really only an infant three months old, and so you will be expecting to hear very little indeed from me to-night.

" But I'm glad to be speaking and speaking as a new-comer and on behalf of the other newcomers here.

" First of all, I want to say how tremendously proud I am to have at last joined this organisation, and to feel that I am taking some part—even though it's still a very small part indeed—in the running of it. Of course, I'm far from being a mechanic yet. In fact, I'm still the chap that passes the tools to the man that passes the tools to the man that's actually doing the job. However, there is some talk of me getting a rise soon, and then I'll be the chap that actually passes the tools to the man that's doing the job.

"I also want to tell you how proud I am to be getting to know all of you. I want to get to know each one in this business individually, and whether I am working under you or with you, or whether you are working for me, I want to know each one of you as a friend.

" Finally, I want to say how tremendously I appreciate and value the way everyone has been so willing to help me in every way possible since I joined up last September, and I should like to thank you all very sincerely for the welcome into this organisation, and for the flying start that you have given me."

The Christmas holiday again found him active in his beloved ski racing, this time in international events at Scheidegg in the Oberland. In the Duke of Kent's Cup he ran sixth of 117 competitors from Switzerland, Italy, Hungary and Great Britain, and followed this up by winning, in a blinding snowstorm, first place in the "Roberts of Kandahar," the oldest and best-known British Downhill ski race. As the British Ski Year Book said he "thus joined the long list of famous British racers whose names appear on this cup." The actual cup is of silver and enormous size and reposes at Murren. A replica adorns the lounge at home.

Practising next day for the British Championship and trying a risky new route down the famous Bumps to gain a split second of time in the race to follow, he took off in a big jump and came down over a boulder strewn path, dislocating his right elbow. That finished his racing for that holiday, but not his ski-ing in which he continued to keep up in the party's ordinary tours with one arm in a sling and with one ski-stick.

As a result of the year's successes he was one of those awarded the highest honours of the year—the Club Colours of the Ski Club of Great Britain, and the Club's Gold Badge for Downhill Ski-Racing, and so seemed likely to achieve his final ski-ing ambition of competing in the classic F.I.S. and Olympic Games for Britain, but the international situation forbade. The return home found the war clouds gathering. The national call to voluntary service was made and Geoffrey at once responded by joining the Supplementary Reserve of Officers in the R.A.S.C. whose duties corresponded most closely to his motor training and vocation. Along with the senior staff at the depot of Appleyard of Leeds Ltd. he took his part in the voluntary nightly lecture courses at the works, which by the middle of the year had trained one thousand territorials in the maintenance and repair of army motor vehicles.

Before the storm broke he had one last opportunity to gratify his passion for the great sport of the snow. The Norwegian Government sent him an invitation to take out a team of British men and women skiers to renew, in the Easter holidays, the happy contests with the Norsemen. Once again he found Norway an exaltation. He wrote from Spiterstulen: " This incredible weather spell continues and we literally haven't seen a cloud in the sky for a fortnight. There is no wind and so it's very hot indeed—for the past four days I've skied without a shirt (even on the top of some of Norway's highest peaks) and only had to put on my shirt when I felt to be getting too burnt. All our faces must be absolutely unrecognisable, we are so exceptionally brown. I am very fit indeed— never been so fit I think in my life, and to-day I have done something I have long wanted to do—that is climbed on ski over 10,000 feet in the day ! A Norwegian and I thought that as a stunt we would like to climb Norway's two highest mountains in one day, so we did the Galdhopiggen this morning starting at 9 a.m., back here for lunch, then the Glittertind this afternoon, getting back at 7 p.m. to Spiterstulen. This meant 10,050 feet of climbing and about 35 kilometres of walking. I don't feel the least bit tired or stiff to-night and feel quite fresh. It seems to be regarded as quite a feat here and doesn't seem to have been done before. We climbed the 5,000 feet from here to the top of 9,000 feet Galdhopiggen in under $2\frac{1}{2}$ hours. Glittertind is about 50 feet higher than Galdhopiggen this year owing to an exceptionally thick ice-cap.

PLATE I

Geoffrey—School Days

By courtesy of Bacon and Ismay Taylor
Also for Frontispiece

" The tour ended yesterday with our arrival here. I can in no way tell you what this tour has meant to me. All I can say is that it has been the most wonderful ski-ing experience I have ever had, and that's an inadequate way of expressing it. To-morrow night a party of us are going to climb to the top of Galdhopiggen in the late afternoon, see the sun set over the Jotunheim at 7-15 p.m., have supper in the shelter there, and then descend the 5,000 feet on the return by the light of the full moon. It should be glorious. This will be our last ' fling ' before serious training for the races. Reider Anderson, the Norwegian jumping champion (and world champion) has just arrived by moonlight. He doesn't seem to be able to stop remarking how brown I am, so I must be quite a good colour ! "

One of the team was Dave Bradley, an American student then at Cambridge. He wrote a graphic account of the tour for the *American Ski Annual*, from which the following is extracted : " We were an Oxford-Cambridge ski team of seven, preparing for races with a team from western Norway. Geoffrey Appleyard, or 'Applicot' as the Norskis called him, was certainly our fastest runner. As I watched this Yorkshire fellow streaking for the valley like a wishbone astride a couple of thunderbolts, my more cautious nature kept reminding me of Kipling's sage remark that only ' mad goats and Englishmen would schuss a thing like that ! '

" The races came all too soon, and on a day when the sun had decided to lie abed in his eiderdown of clouds. No light ; no contours in the snow ; no shadows by which to tell the smooth snow from the stretches of wind-waves. As we stood at the top most of us were

----

PLATE II

University Days—Cambridge
Caius College First Boat about to "bump" their rivals
Geoffrey rowing number seven

By courtesy of Stearn & Sons, Cambridge

B

perplexed as to the best way to navigate that frozen tempest between the second and the third controls. 'I'm going to take my skis off and walk down that bit on crampons,' was the honest conclusion.

" However, the Norwegian who started first dictated the course for the rest of us. Down the first schuss he went, gaining speed all the way to the second control ; then a turn right and a straight line down that three hundred yards of white water with the sound of an express train going over a bridge. He skidded perilously close to a reef of rocks beyond the third control, and then straightened out down the long slope and disappeared in the gully. That was nearly half of the course. Beyond the gully one comes out on a high bluff that is like a couple of sixty meter hills placed one on top of the other. Losing altitude at the rate of five hundred feet in fifteen seconds, one is fairly hurled down the last gentler slope to the finish on the lake.

" One by one the competitors poled off, and then crouched for speed ; one by one, almost to a second they disappeared into the gully. Then my turn came, my own ' Fem . . . fir . . . tre . . . to . . . en . . . GO ! '—and suddenly the race was over. The speed being infinite, there was no separation between starting and finishing ; if Einstein had been a skier he would have understood this long ago. No, that two thousand foot drop, that minute and a half, was just one prolonged moment ; and in that half-light, a moment of falling through a hurricane cloud.

" Three runners were not so lucky as the rest ; they skidded off the bluff, tumbled through some low brush, and dropped fifteen feet into a little rock-strewn ravine. But you can't hurt a Norski. Geoffrey and Tim were the winners, tying for first with an average speed of well over fifty miles an hour, which frequently entailed a speed of over a mile a minute."

Ski-ing in Norway is the national sport and in the newspapers receives the prominence football and cricket do in England, whilst such an international event as the above is the equivalent of a Test Match in

England. The race was described under seven column banner headlines emphasizing the success of the English captain against Norway together with photographs of " Den Engelske vinner av utforrennet Geoffrey Appleyard, lederen av troppen." The race was considered by the Norwegian papers as quite outstanding and the speed of the winners as sensational.

Dave Bradley continues : " So the Vatnahalsrennet was done for 1939. We packed our rucksacks carefully, putting all but the most necessary equipment into suitcases to be sent to Oslo, for the coming week was to bring the great adventure : the trip through the Sognefjord, followed by six days of ski-ing across the Jotunheim. That night Geoffrey gave us our marching song :—

Hi ho, hi ho, through the Jotunheim we go,
With skis and packs and klister wax, hi ho, hi ho.

This Norwegian picture might well conclude with a sonnet written by Dave Bradley commemorating the finish of a five hours' climb of Mount Fanaroken with Geoffrey. A blizzard of blowing particles of ice had faced them all the way until towards the very end they saw the cabin upon the peak against the blaze of a flaming sunset :—

Half frozen then—for that sub-zero blast
Brought all the cold in barren Jotunheim—
We leaned upon our poles. The trek was ended,
The Hut, a chimneyed drift, ahead at last,
Where weird snow shapes in frozen pantomime
Looked on. Bold Day and stealthy Night
contended
In the clouds, and North and South the vast
Range glowed like turrets of a Fort defended.
Awhile the sky was overwhelmed with light ;
But Night was yet supreme, if Day sublime :
One by one the flaming battlements
Were quenched. Then in the gusts the rich incense
Of burning Birch ! The Hut ! We turned to climb,
Nor saw the blue East thicken into night.

DAVE BRADLEY.

CHAPTER II

WAR! WITH THE B.E.F.

IN AUGUST THE call came for the mobilisation of the Supplementary Reserve of Officers. Geoff reported to Salisbury Plain. It was the hottest part of the year. One day, his men were digging trenches in the heat of the mid-day sun and their efforts flagged. He stripped to the waist and dug with them, and they mightily improved. A senior officer came along and seeing no officer in charge asked where he was. " I'm here, sir," said Geoff, stripped, in the bottom of a trench. The reprimand was severe in regard to being improperly dressed and in conduct unbecoming an officer. The incident coloured Geoff's view of Army discipline throughout his career. He had been used to working with his mechanics in his business and sharing their difficulties and took a " poor view " of the Red Tab's ideas of leadership. But on 18/9/39 he wrote enthusiastically of his new job.

" So, I'm now O.C. ' E ' Section. This means I have 45 men (nearly all skilled men, mechanics, fitters, turners, electricians, blacksmiths, carpenters, coppersmiths, etc.) and 8 vehicles of my own. There are 2 breakdowns, 2 stores vans, 2 mobile workshops (marvellous vehicles—10 tons each and fitted with electrically driven lathe, drill, etc.) and 2 spares lorries. Also, of course, my private car (2-door Ford Prefect, sunshine roof) and a motor cycle. I have the responsibility of looking after the 160 or so vehicles of the entire Company—also 20 motor cycles."

Then came the news of the Russian pact with Germany. " So Russia is in. How awful. And what a swinish thing to do. It means a long war, but I'm sure we must win. I'm certain we've got right on our side and I even feel we've got God on our side—if God could conceivably be on any side in anything so bloody as a war. We *must* win. Funny how relative everything is—you don't really appreciate a holiday till it's over. The same way you don't really appreciate your liberty until it's threatened. But I'll *never* be made to say ' Heil Hitler.' I'd sooner die.

" Life has been too busy to worry about anything. What a ' day of rest ' Sunday is in the Army—when at war ! We started work to-day at 8 a.m. and knocked off at 6 p.m. Still, that was shorter than the normal day nowadays as we normally work till sundown. I must get to bed. I'm feeling rather lousy after the injections and I've to get up at 6 a.m. to-morrow as I am camp orderly officer for the day and have to meet and inspect the guards and sentries, inspect the men's mess, etc., and generally get blamed for anything in the camp that goes wrong. Goodnight to you all, dearest love, Geoff."

Soon after this he was at sea amongst the first of the British Expeditionary Force in one of the early convoys to sail for France. To his sister, Margot, he wrote :—

"At sea off Land's End, ss. *Lady of Mann.* I don't know if this will ever reach you. I am going to bribe one of the crew to take it back to England on this ship and post it. Things are going very well with me and I have ' inner peace ' in spite of the war without. The average Tommy is a great-hearted chap and we get on famously. Much as I dislike a lot of things in the Army, it really is an amazing brotherhood of men and there is some sort of team spirit in it that must get a tremendous grip on you in time. Also I am very lucky in this Company with my fellow officers. The boys are an incredibly cheerful crowd and it takes a lot to make them grumble. For instance, on this ship they are packed like sardines (1,500 on each ship, and the ships are smaller than cross-channel boats), they are sleeping out on deck fully clothed with only a great-coat and one blanket (and it's not warm), the food is plain and there doesn't seem to be unlimited quantity of it, and yet they are singing heartily and seem thoroughly cheerful. And if you ask them how things are going they tell you ' we're doing fine, sir ! '

"Also an amazing thing to me is that they don't seem to have any resentment at all towards the officers. As you know, we live a lot more comfortably than the men, we eat better, we don't get up as early (except when on orderly duty) and altogether have a lot better time of it. And yet they don't seem to grudge it at all, but accept it as quite normal. I'm sure that I should feel awfully resentful about it—after all, we are all in the Army and we are at war !

" I got a tremendous kick out of something that happened the other day, just before leaving Bulford. You remember I was changed over from being O.C. of ' D ' section to ' E ' section (workshops). After two days of the change my sergeant in ' D ' section approached me and said he had had about half the section asking him if they could transfer to ' E ' section. Of course it couldn't be done, but it was a great thrill to know that when you do try and get to know the men and take their point of view and fix things for them as you would like them yourself, that they appreciate it. It does make it really worth while to get to know men individually, and I'm certain it must make a difference when we have a job of work to do later on, although the Army doesn't seem to approve of it. But somehow I feel that in the Army you can get to know your troops and still retain the officer and men relationship without it being ' familiar.'

" Of course, may be the men in ' D ' section merely wanted to change to ' E ' as they thought they had a soft officer !

" There was a troops' concert just before we left Bulford. A great occasion. Some excellent turns were done, too. Also community singing—all the grand old songs—' Tipperary,' ' Pack up your troubles,' ' Land of hope and glory,' etc.—all being sung by over 1,000 men packed into a tent. Golly, it was impressive. It gave me a queer sort of thrill to look round the hundreds of faces in the dimly-lit tent and hear those grand songs go swelling up. The same sort of ' queer thrill ' you get when you hear a lovely piece of music sometimes. But there was something indefinable that was awfully sad about it. May be it was the thought that somewhere not so very far away there would be a crowd of German lads, just the same great-hearted chaps, singing the same sort of patriotic songs and also wondering what on earth we are going to war with each other about !

" What a hell of a lot of wasted patriotism war means.

" I am afraid we are in for a dirty night. Now we are round the corner a strong wind has got up. A lot of the troops are on the forward deck ' spray dodging ' and further aft I note that people are already beginning to be ill. What fun, with every inch of deck space already taken up for sleeping. Poor devils !

" I have just come off the boat deck with a very spray-wet face and am going to have a meal and then early to bed. I suppose we shall get into the ' Bay ' in about eight hours. Well, old dear, keep grinning. I'll be thinking of you doing your bit. Dearest love, and God bless and keep you."

By the middle of October he was beginning to get restive for action. " There is a general feeling here that this temporary calm will shortly be broken when (and if) Hitler invades Holland or Belgium, and we are almost hourly expecting orders for a sudden move up and forward towards the frontier. I wonder if you heard Churchill's speech last night. I expect you did. Wasn't it terrific ! Straight from the shoulder. I bet it's made old Hitler pretty livid, to be told quite so plainly just what kind of a blackguard he is ! "

His experiences moving up to the Front in France from the port of disembarkation were very varied, thus : " With the arrival at this village quite a lot of the fun has gone out of this war. Quite suddenly, winter has come with a bang, and there is mud everywhere. Mud, mud, mud wherever you go. It rains off and on all through the day and the sky is heavy, misty and over-cast. Cheerful prospect! The village here is much smaller than Linton and consists solely of farms. The men are billeted in the farm buildings (hay lofts, etc.), the officers one each in the farms. I have a room in a very broken down farm. It is a single room not connected with the house, and opens direct on to the farm yard manure heap where the pigs and hens grub for food. The room has no window at all or any other inlet except for the door. So if I want light other than artificial I have to leave the door wide open and allow the hens, etc., to come in and out! Still, I'm a lot better off than the men as at least I've got a bed to sleep on and a roof overhead. The first night here my men were billeted in a cowshed—absolutely filthy. To add to the fun about 6 p.m. the cows started to make their way back to the mangers and attempted to take possession. For some time the issue as to the result of the conflict was in doubt, but finally my gallant men won and the cows were repelled! Apparently the farmer intended that men and cows should sleep together on the same straw. However, I have now got alternative billets for my men in the chateau coach-house which are a lot better. At any rate, it is dry and clean and when I have managed to get some palliasses so that the men have something on which to sleep between them and the concrete we shall be quite comfortable.''

Then by contrast : '' On the way up, one night we couldn't possibly catch the column that night as we were towing some loaded lorries (ammunition) and therefore were forbidden to travel after dark. At dusk we stopped in a French country town about the size of Wetherby. I went to find the Mayor (it's quite the thing to do) and in half an hour's time he had every man in my section in civilian billets! The people took us into their houses (two men in each house) and were incredibly good to us. Every man slept between sheets (for the first time for six weeks) and had a fine dinner and breakfast. Of course they were as pleased as Punch.

Some even had their boots cleaned for them by the maids of the houses ! !   Being an officer I was treated like a king and stayed the night and dined with the local big noise—a Monsieur Decantelle who spoke faultless English.   When we parted he gave me a magnificent many-tool, rustless clasp knife which will have multiple uses.   It has certainly been a week of contrasts—one night in a hayloft, the next in a chateau, then in a farm house, and then a night in the back of a lorry !   The people have given us a grand welcome. Everywhere we have been they have brought us masses of flowers and fruit—peaches, grapes, apples and pears absolutely without end.   And then when we have halted by the roadside for mid-day meals, they have brought out extra food, wine, cider, etc.   And they wouldn't take a sou in payment."

As winter came nearer he was thinking of the snow again.   " The Ski Club Year Book has come—it is grand to have that, and I shall eagerly read every word of it.   But it certainly makes me long for and look forward to the time when I shall again clip over my Kandahar bindings and hear the race-starter saying ' three, two, one, GO ' ! !   Attaboy !   I do hope the German cracks Lautschner, Willi Walch, Clausing, Reiser and others don't get killed in this blasted war because they are such ' maestros.'   What a crazy business this war is !   I don't ever want to get the better of those chaps—except in a ski race."

And then another memory of pre-war years :   " I had rather an experience the other day.   I was passing very near the Canadian Memorial (which we can see from this village) on one of my trips out in the car for supplies, so thought I would stop and renew my acquaintance with it.   It certainly is a fine thing, but now a lot of it is shielded up for protection, including all the statues and the long list of carved names all over it.   However, it was rather an experience to stand in front of it again and cast my mind back to the time I was there last, returning from one of those happy

summer tours ! Little did I think then that the next
time I should see it I should be wearing my own tin
hat and my own revolver strapped by my side. What
a tragedy that it may all happen again.

"So the air raids on England have really started.
Now that there has been this attack on the Firth of
Forth and on Scapa Flow the balloon has gone right
up, and we may soon expect real happenings ! Hurrah !
Let's get to it, and get it settled."

By the end of October things were becoming more
static. He says : " I am beginning to know the local
countryside very well—it is interesting because of its
associations with the last war. The name of every
village, town and hill and ridge is a familiar one !
Jimmy goes with me everywhere and he is an excellent
companion, a good batman, and a fair driver. In fact,
his constant attendance on me is becoming rather a
joke amongst my fellow officers, and he is often referred
to as my shadow ! We get on very well together and
are great pals. Also he knows when he ought to produce the ' yes, sirs ' and the salutes and discipline that
the ' soldier speaking to officer ' relationship demands
and when he can behave and talk to me like a normal
human being, that is when we are alone in the car. So
all is very satisfactory there.

"The weather now ! I can hardly describe it
calmly. In fact, only its extreme coldness keeps me
from becoming very heated about it ! ! It really is
behaving abominably—to-day and yesterday we have
had snow at intervals and heavy rain almost continually.
In the past ten days we have had two days on which we
had occasional glimpses of the sun just to let us see
that it still really existed, but the rest have been cold
and damp and very wintry with frost at night. And
it's still only October. What a delightful country !
The mud now of course is overwhelming and beyond
comment.

"Last Sunday I managed to get to service—the first
I have managed since mobilisation. The service was
held in the little schoolroom in this village and only

about 70 men were able to go due to lack of accommodation. It was a grand, simple service conducted by the padre and very touching. I was tremendously glad to have the opportunity of going but it was a very sober congregation that trooped out. When the padre prayed for the comforting and safety of you all at home I somehow felt very close to you and could just picture you all probably in the little chapel at Wetherby, and I almost was with you for a little time. And I think the whole congregation felt very much the same as they thought of their parents and wives and kiddies and brothers and sisters. Still, *c'est la guerre !* The padre is attached to the Ammunition Park and is with us permanently. A very good chap—his home is Skye ! By the way, our time is still the same as yours.

" The word on everyone's lips now is ' leave.' Apparently some lucky ones will get home for Christmas. In any case we should all get two weeks leave within the next six months so that really is something to look forward to. Of course, as soon as I get any idea when I may get leave I'll let you know. But don't be too hopeful yet awhile. Meantime I'm in first-class health. The padre says the reason I look so fit is that I eat so much—apparently he likes men about him who eat heartily. The raising of my messing subscription is already under discussion, I'm afraid."

His letter of 8/11/39 to his schoolboy brother gave details calculated to be interesting. "Well, we still haven't seen Hitler yet. No bombs, no gas, no nothing, which is all very dull. However, Jerry's planes keep popping over occasionally now (apparently reconnaissance) and most of them get brought down. I was over at an aerodrome (R.A.F.) a few miles from here two days ago ; the boys there were in great spirits as they had that day brought down three planes—their ' first blood ' of the war.

" I've been getting a certain amount of weapon training which is really good fun (most of it) and can hardly be called work. I'm not too bad with a revolver now and can guarantee to hit a man's head at 20 yards, which is supposed to be pretty fair. Have been firing the Bren too—it's a wizard little toy ! Absolutely dead accurate and simple sighting. It's grand to aim and press the trigger, hear her spit and kick five rounds out, and then put your glasses on the target and find you've riddled the bull. It certainly is a beautiful weapon to handle.

" But there is one weapon that I never want to have to fire again—nor does anyone. That is the anti-tank rifle. It's the most filthy weapon to fire that ever was.

" The weapon is like an enormous rifle and has a barrel about 4ft. long and so is incredibly accurate. I managed the best shot of the day with my second shot and was plumb through the centre of the bull at 200 yards. But it's mighty difficult to concentrate on sighting and firing when you know the kick it is going to give your shoulder when you touch that trigger ! "

A letter written on 13/11/39 commented on a curious optimism which the Home Front apparently felt at that date. " There is a very firm confidence everywhere here as regards the strength of our position in this war. I too feel that there can be no question about its ultimate result in favour of the Allies. But no one here thinks it will be over before Xmas as some people appear to think. It won't. But we'll be ski-ing again a year hence ! I heard on the wireless to-night that the Olympic games are now cancelled. Well, maybe there will be a chance of another yet. I notice rather rue-fully in my diary that to-morrow night I should be at the dinner at Grosvenor House of the Ski Club of Great Britain to have team colours for 1939 presented to me and also the Gold Downhill Ski Racing Badge. I wonder if the dinner is still being held. I have seen no notice to the contrary."

A little later Jerry was beginning to show signs of life. " There have been big sabotage scares here lately as the enemy is said to have dropped (or to be going to drop) sabotage squads by parachute during the night from planes. They then do all the sabotage they can and finally give themselves up. We of course provide a most excellent opportunity for sabotage and so very strict precautions are being taken. All night guards on vehicles and ammunition dumps have been doubled and so we have about 80 guards and sentries out each night now. And what a game for the orderly officer who has to inspect them. It means two complete rounds a night all over the countryside and takes nearly two hours each round. I do my first round between 10 and 12, then to bed for 2½ hours, then a round between 3 and 5, another hour in bed, and then another day's work. Orderly officer comes round every fourth day, and we don't look forward to it. I always take a loaded revolver round with me and it has a comforting feel. I haven't had to use it in earnest yet but I've several times had my finger on the trigger when investigating outlying farm buildings, haystacks, ditches, etc., where a sentry reports he has seen or heard something suspicious. And when it's a pitch dark night, raining and with a driving wind at 3 a.m. it can be quite eerie and ' nervy ' so that a gun in your fist is a real comfort ! No, being orderly officer is not much of a picnic.

"Also the guards tend to get a bit jumpy when they are on a lonely beat by themselves. I'm quite scared of getting shot by one as they only challenge once ' Halt, who goes there ' and if they receive no answer, they shoot ! And if you are some distance away sloshing through mud with the wind whistling in your ears and rain falling it is easy to miss the challenge ! The last night I was on duty I found one very indignant sentry ! Another guard on a different beat had challenged him from 80 yards away, but he hadn't heard it and so had not replied, and the other guard had whipped up his rifle and taken a shot at him ! However the aim wasn't good as it was a pitch dark filthy night and the bullet missed and struck a wall behind him off which, to use the guard's own words ' the bullet ricocheted like a streak of white-hot metal ' ! He was very, vexed that another guard should have taken a pot at him and took a very sickly view of the whole affair. I examined the wall where the bullet struck—it had removed a very pretty lump of stone ! Actually I was rather in favour of the occurrence—it will keep the guards on their toes.

" Well, I must away. I'm very fit and well—no colds or anything. My only complaint is lack of sleep of which I only get about an average of 5 hours each 24— and you know I can accommodate 12 ! Still, it isn't really bothering me, although I don't feel very fresh first thing in the morning. I'm not learning to love this mud-soaked corner of Europe any more—it must be the most utterly God-forsaken piece of land in the world. Did someone say something about ' La *Belle* France ' ? I prefer ' La Bl. . . . . . France.'

" I had quite a light day last Sunday—in the morning I marched 100 men $3\frac{1}{2}$ miles to a village near here ($3\frac{1}{2}$ miles each way !) to church parade. It was very much of a ' blood and thunder, punishment ' sort of sermon, and I felt quite like telling the preacher that that wasn't my idea of a Christian God, but I didn't think it would go down very well. He said some absurd things including that death, illness, financial misfortunes, etc., were a direct visitation on one for one's sins ! A lot of poppycock, I thought, and I should like to have told the assembled congregation that too ! Still the march there and back was fun and all the old favourite marching songs were sung—' Tipperary,' ' Keep the home fires burning,' etc. There was good support for the dance favourite ' South of the Border ' and weak support for ' There'll always be an England,' but actually the new patriotic songs haven't yet caught on at all over here—whatever the papers tell you.

" One thing that infuriates the boys more than any-thing over here, is when they get letters from home saying ' I suppose you were at this and that concert,' etc., or else ' I see from the papers that you are having a marvellous time out there.' Apparently the papers

are making out that life here is one colossal party!
But not in this unit! Of course living under officer's
conditions I haven't got any grumbles, but it isn't such
a bed of roses here for the troops, and they don't like
to think that people in England are hearing that they
are having the time of their lives! Things are deadly
monotonous (less so for my section having a trades-
man's job to do, though), billets are only moderate (my
men sleep on a stone floor but are warm and dry), food
is really good (no complaints at all), but it's a hard
life for all. And there aren't any feather beds, concert
parties (except the boys' own ones), or cushy jobs for
anyone.

" One of my friends saw the C. in C. the other day,
which was rather alarming! Hope I don't run into
Tiger Gort—I'd be scared stiff and dry in the mouth.
The C. in C.!! Actually I hear that he met some
of our company lads in ———— to-day in the street. He
stopped them and asked them who they were, and if
they were enjoying life, good food, etc. Actually I
should think he's rather a good egg.

" What do you think of Russia's latest ? Attacking
and bombing Finland—lousy!

" I just can't weigh up what's happening (or what is
likely to happen) at all. The issue seems most confused and far reaching now. And why aren't they
getting on with the war ? Things get more and more
peaceful here. That is as regards war-like activities.
We haven't even had a plane over for days.

" But there is an infuriating lot of waste work being
done in this darned war. It's very much a ' paper '
war and the amount of correspondence and letters and
memorandums, etc., that go through my hands daily is
crazy. In fact, everything is reverting to a peace-time
basis out here and it's all very fiddling and aggravating.
I often wish a good sized bomb could drop near this
chateau and just make people realise that a war is on,
and that really Workshops' one and only job that really

matters is to put vehicles on the road by hook or by crook and keep them there."

In the middle of December 1939 he was offered a move to the Ammunition Section, giving better chances of promotion, but told the C.O. he would prefer to stay in Workshops where he was perfectly happy with his men who were having to work harder and longer than the Ammunition Section. He wrote : " I know I have the men right behind me because on several occasions I've had to call for volunteers for men to do a job on some particularly filthy night when the last thing the men wanted to do was to turn out and grovel in a ditch under a lorry, and every time every man's hand has gone up as a volunteer."

Nevertheless, two weeks later the Colonel moved him on. He was not enthusiastic about starting all over again at the bottom learning a new job and new men. He wrote : " I had a very pleasant and unexpected surprise just as I was leaving to come over here—my sergeant asked me if I'd mind stepping up to the Workshops to have a word with the men who were all clustered together up there and they presented me with a lovely leather-bound zip-fastener travelling writing case for which they had all clubbed together and bought me. Wasn't it grand of them, as they only get a frightfully meagre rate of pay anyway ? Of course it was a very unmilitary thing to do and strictly against King's Regulations. A court martial offence, I believe !

--- --- --- --- --- --- --- ---

Plate IIIa

Caius College Eight May's Boat, 1938
Geoffrey (captain) centre

By courtesy of Hills & Saunders, Cambridge

Plate IIIb

Geoffrey—a Norwegian snap taken when ski-touring

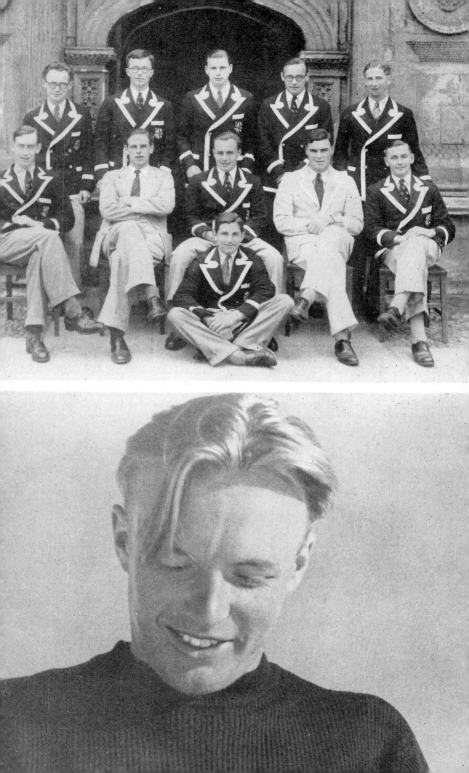

" I moved over here a week ago, and actually, as it's turned out, it was definitely a move for the good in the long run except for the one important thing that I'm now out of Workshops. I am going to find the job of Ammunition Officer fascinating—it really is mighty interesting. It consists in principle of working in close liaison with the gunners, knowing and anticipating what their demands are likely to be in advance and, at the other end, knowing what is available at railhead, where it is, etc. It entails knowing as much as possible about all the different kinds of ammunition and explosives used, also how they are used, who uses them, equivalent loads, fuses, cartridges, etc., etc. Added to the interest of the job is the excellent chance of promotion that it offers."

On 22/12/39 he wrote : " Well, I had quite a change for my birthday—and quite a rest too, which has done me a lot of good. I felt lousy (not literally) on the afternoon of the 19th and went to bed about 4-30 with a bit of a chill (or 'flu) and a temperature of just over 100°. Actually it has been quite a pleasant rest and I'm feeling a lot fitter now than I was a week ago. Ready once more for the rigours (?) of modern warfare ! But I'm rather annoyed at spoiling my own record as, except for broken bones, I reckon this is the first time for seven years that I've retired to bed with a cold or illness. Yes, Mummy, I know you'll be saying that I ought to have gone a dozen times in the past but was too obstinate.

" But this time a temperature seemed a reasonable excuse for going to bed and, anyway, the doctor ordered it so there was no choice. Still, it was a pity to break

--- --- --- --- --- --- --- ---

PLATE IV

Geoff and other Light Blues show their paces
Taken whilst practising for the Oxford-Cambridge
'Varsity Race, 1937

By courtesy of Charles F. Brown, F.I.B.P.

that record. . . . It has been very cold here all day—13° F. below freezing point on the thermometer outside the door. Quite Swiss-like temperatures. My wireless has been a great boon whilst in bed—and there was a glorious programme this morning—a sound broadcast from Eskdale and Wastdale! How I loved it! I never realised before that Lakeland sheep (Herdwicks) have a ' baa ' all their own. Instantly I heard a sheep ' baa ' over the wireless this morning my mind jumped straight to the Lake District. I don't think the sheep anywhere else make quite the same noise! The programme took the form of a girl walking through Eskdale and over to Wastdale, including sound recordings of people she met on the way, the Lakeland hunt, mountain streams, and best of all, the calling of the curlew! Oh joy! It really was an inspired programme, quite genuine recordings I'm certain, and to all who know and love the Lakes, and that region of them in particular, it was a real delight. Especially to those far away from them. Rather wonderful, out here in France, to hear sounds from Cumberland. It made me feel very homesick for the hills! I must stop. Batman Jimmy (who acts as my nurse) says it's time for me to go to bed and that I've been up long enough (it's 7-30 p.m.—got up at 2 p.m.). He's the dickens of a bully in such matters in spite of his small stature! "

Jimmy, by the way, thought so much of his officer that when he heard the great news that he was the father of a baby boy he insisted the child should be called 'Alastair Geoffrey.' His Aberdeenshire home people protested that there never had been such a name as Geoffrey in their family, but that didn't matter to Jimmy—' Geoffrey ' it had to be and ' Geoffrey ' it was.

On Christmas Eve Geoff wrote : " Merry Christmas to you all ! I'll be thinking of home to-night and imagining the ceremony of hanging up the stockings in the dining-room, followed by the furtive creeping round by members of the family putting into the stockings their various gifts ! I do hope my Christmas parcel has arrived in time. Of course, this Christmas at home will be another real children's Christmas, I suppose, as you have three evacuees. What fun—I guess the kids have the time of their lives ! I shall hang up my stocking here to-night, but I have no reason at all to suppose that I shall not take it down again in the morning equally empty ! Still putting it up is a gesture, anyway ! However, I too will be opening my parcels in the morning, as a most enormously heavy and interesting looking parcel arrived here for me—I think from home—last night. With enormous self-control I refrained from opening it on arrival, and so I shall open it with great excitement to-morrow !

" I wonder if you are having Christmassy weather at home ? It still continues very cold here (the thermometer hasn't been above freezing point for 10 days now) and the countryside is white over with a blanket of hoar frost. To-day has been very foggy all day and consequently with the roads getting wet, to-night they are absolutely a sheet of ice and almost undrivable. Luckily I was orderly officer last night, and so escape the Christmas nights as I shan't be on again until the 27th. It was a most glorious night last night— brilliantly clear, white frost everywhere, and an almost full moon—so I made my tour of the guards on foot for the pleasure of walking on such a lovely night—it took me two hours, but it was worth walking. I'm getting quite a bit of walking now as it's the only possible form of exercise.

" Christmas Eve—I can't help remembering that Christmas Eve three years ago—the best day I ever spent on ski I think. It was the day three of us skied over from Breuil to Zermatt and back again—the trip for which we couldn't get a guide as they said it couldn't be done in a day ! We left Zermatt to cross back over the Theodul Pass at 4 p.m., just as it was getting dark. Then there was a memorable two hours climbing to the Schwarzsee where the moon came out, and then an unforgettable three hours up the glacier, with the Matterhorn, drenched in white clinging snow and in the full moonlight standing right over us on the right hand, seeming almost on top of us ; dead ahead was the Breithorn, and away to the left Monte Rosa and its glaciers. We were up at 11,500 ft. on top of the Theodul at 10 p.m. (and was it cold !) and then an hour later were down in Breuil 5,500 ft. below. It was a glorious trip.

"At this exact time—6-30—I guess we would be halting at the Schwarzsee. I remember we had some chocolate and tried to get warm, as we had been banking on the hotel being open and on getting a hot meal there !

" I've been eagerly searching the newspapers and illustrated papers for snow and ski-ing pictures, but without avail. It does seem a pity that when we can't get the proper thing, the papers don't rally round and dig up the usual winter sports pictures just to remind one that such things do still exist !

" We have each had a Greetings card from the King and Queen—a very nice one consisting of a card with their photos on one side, and on the other ' With our best wishes for Christmas, 1939. May God bless and protect you ' in natural writing, and signed ' Elizabeth R ' and ' George R.I.'

" I went over to 6 Sub-Park this morning to have a word with the men in Workshops and wish them a merry Christmas, and found that they had made me a beautiful mahogany coffee table as a Christmas present. Wasn't it ripping of them ! It's beautifully done with a lovely grain and polished naturally without stain. The legs are spiral cut (like the dining-room chairs) and were made by the turners, the table itself was made by the carpenters and the polishing and finishing were done by the painters—so in one way or another, nearly everyone in the Workshops had a go at some part of it ! It's a lovely thing and it is fun to have it as it was made in the Field. But I haven't the foggiest idea of how I'll get it home *après la guerre*.

" By the way, did you notice that the other day you sent me an invitation to Peggy's wedding reception—well, mow me down, I didn't even know she was engaged ! You know it's a bit thick, dozens of the nicest girls are getting married in England at present and here are we stagnating out here and unable to do anything about it ! It isn't good enough ! I take a very sickly view of it ! The time flies until I shall be coming home. I reckon I ought to be at home four weeks to-day. Oh, boy, oh, boy ! "

Another move temporarily to H.Q. took place early in 1940, but he was getting restive for action. " You will doubtless be interested to know that this town was the German G.H.Q. *dans la guerre de quatorze* and that Field Marshal Hindenburg lived for six months in the bedroom I have here and in which I am now writing ! ! General's luxury, motor cars, H.Q., comfortable billets—I'm a fine soldier ! I must go to bed. I'm very tired and rather fed up. It's rather sickening to get landed into this luxury job ! "

Then followed a wonderful fortnight's home leave and on his return a letter in which he gave the news of a momentous change in his life. " You know that grand hymn ' Once to every man and nation comes the moment to decide '—well, that moment to decide has come to me and the day I left home and the night I spent in London I made the great decision that I shall never regret, I know—that of giving my life to Christ.

" I haven't necessarily joined the Oxford Group although I believe that in time this will mean full identification with them. But I have decided that I have tried running my own life on my own principles and standards long enough and not made a very startling success of it. So now I am going to run my life on God's standards and in the way He wants me to run it and so try and do my bit in the remaking and moral rearmament of the world.

"And it's going to mean a lot of changes in my life. I don't know quite how much I have deceived you both as to the real kind of fellow I am, but I know that I have 'acted' so successfully in the past that a lot of people think I'm quite a sound chap who has apparently made quite a success of things so far. Whereas actually large areas of my life have been a gigantic bluff and very few people know how completely selfish my life has been up till now.

" I've failed miserably and continually on all Christ's standards of honesty, purity, unselfishness and love. And so now I am going to surrender all my thoughts and actions to God in the certain knowledge that I, under His control, can make a far, far better job of my life, and do far more with my life, than I ever possibly could without it.

" One of the things that has 'changed' me more than anything is the realisation of the amazing amount of love there is in our house and the tremendous amount of love that you both pour out for us. And then on top of that the realisation of how little I was really capable of reciprocating that love and being worthy of it because of the way I was completely wrapped up in my own selfish ideals and thoughts. This has been brought home to me on this last leave more than ever before, and I do thank you both very, very much for the love you have shown me and for the love that there is in our home.

"Another great cause of my change of heart is the unfailing and never-tiring love that Garth and others have always showed me, and the grand witness of their own lives. I feel too as though I have let Margot down long enough, have let her stand on her own long enough, through not having had the courage to take this step before. And I'm tremendously grateful for the way in which she has always stood by me.

" There's a life's work to do out here ! If I can help to spread a spirit of moral rearmament here to counter the spirit of moral rot there is at present, it may yet be in time to find a solution to the world's problems or at any rate to build a new world when peace comes."

From this time onwards Geoffrey relied greatly on God's guidance and help at all times.

Geoff still kept up his ornithological interests in France. On one occasion he found a dead long-eared owl in a trench and sent it home in a cardboard box. It arrived in a very ' high ' condition but still a good subject for a coloured photograph, which was successfully exhibited by his younger brother at his old school. To him Geoffrey wrote :—

" I heard my first migrant for the year here to-day— a chiff-chaff ! Quite unmistakable—it repeated its chiff-chaffing several times. 'Twas in a wood between the office and here and was in high trees so I couldn't get a glimpse of it. I haven't yet heard the willow warbler which one usually in England seems to get the first of the two. Winter seems so recently finished here (and at times one still doesn't feel quite certain that it is really finished) that it was quite a shock to hear such a summer bird. However in latitude I suppose we are really quite a long way south. I was amazed when I looked at the map and saw that practically the whole of Northern France is further south than Cornwall !—which perhaps explains why the migrants are here so much earlier than they are in Linton. Also to-day in the same wood I found a practically completed nest—either blackbird or song thrush—my first definite new one so far. I was surprised to hear that your birds at home are so very late nesting.

" What a thrilling recovery that was of the starling roosting at York, ringed at Ampleforth ! I think it's the most interesting and original starling recovery Bootham has had. It practically proves the amazing area from which starlings do flock to a communal roost. It gives an explanation of the vast numbers of birds at a roost when you realise they may have collected from an area of radius at least twenty miles round the roost, that is from an area of at least 1,300 square miles !

" Glad you are learning ' To a Waterfowl '—it's a lovely poem. I haven't got it out here, but could recite every word for you ! I love the verse

> * *But soon thy toil shall end*
> *Soon shalt thou find a summer home, and rest,*
> *And scream among thy fellows ;*
> *Reeds shall bend soon o'er thy sheltered nest.*

The last line conjures up Skipwith memories, some-how, and the continual screaming of the blackheads, the smell of the peaty muddy water, wet gym-clothes and warm water ! And then cold meat and salad (soaked in vinegar) at the pub ! "

By April 1940 the ' balloon was beginning to go up ' —and to Geoffrey's indignation, in Norway, his happy hunting ground. He wrote " Poor Norway ! What a swine Hitler is ! It is almost impossible to imagine bombs on Oslo, and then the surrender of Oslo and its occupation by German troops. And Bergen too. Poor Norway and poor Norwegians because they are so fond of their country. At first I was afraid the Germans would sweep straight through the country as they have done through Denmark before the Norskies had a chance to resist. Then it looked as though Norway was going to capitulate and negotiate with Hitler, which would have been an awful tragedy for her (and for us), but now it looks as though she is going to fight for it. And if they do get time to mobilise into some sort of formation I'm sure they can put up a terrific scrap, which will give us time to get an Allied force out there to their aid. I went to see the Brigadier to-night and in view of my knowledge of Norway and my slight (I didn't actually use this latter word) knowledge of Norwegian he has promised to try and get me into any force the Allies may be sending to Norway. But I'm afraid there isn't a lot of hope for me getting there as I suppose any force that is sent will go direct from England. Poor Norway. But I hope she fights until the Germans are very sorry they ever heard of her."

* By M. C. Bryant.

Then a week later : " I should like to be in a ski battalion along with Einer and Arild, Olaf and Otto ! Perhaps I will yet . . . I shall begin urging again when the winter comes !

" My leave prospects are very bright ! There is every chance that I should get home on my original date ; that is, leaving here the 8th May, home 9th, which is sensational."

By the end of April a nostalgic touch : " I am so glad that you have been getting up into the Dales. Your news of those places is very, very welcome to me, and each name conjures up a picture ! Golly, how I miss dear old home and Yorkshire at times in this flat mining countryside ! But the next best thing to being there myself is having your news of these places and to know that you are all enjoying them and that they still exist, and that they will still be the same when the war is over. I shall send my spirit over to dwell in one of the curlews, so, one of the days you are up on the moors, if you see a particularly friendly curlew, you'll know it's me.

" The troops' French is very amusing. I noticed in a letter I was censoring to-day one fellow was making some remark to his pal in England about the French *Madamwazelles*. Letter censoring *is* a curse—how I loathe it ! And it takes up those odd half-hours during the day that one could normally use for one's own correspondence. And fifty or so average letters a day take some getting through. It's an insight into what men are thinking, though. Their attitude to the war, their N.C.O.'s, the officers, etc., and so in those ways is quite useful. Quite often you can find a grouse in a man's letter and put it right by a frank talk with him which otherwise would have been bottled up and never come to light. Although I always try to avoid direct reference to the men to anything I have read in their letters, so as to let them forget as much as possible that everything they write is read and pried into by ' some ruddy orficer.' "

A letter later written by one of Geoffrey's non-commissioned officers, Cpl. L. E. Prout, R.A.S.C., says : " We knew that Apple hated censoring letters and several of us tried a good humoured ' dig ' at the Censor when writing to the girl of the moment. We all had a very good laugh when on leave, for we found that he had very neatly capped our quips and sallies by means of marginal notes, to the great delight of the fair recipients ! "

Hopes of leave were rising high on 25/4/40. " Hurrah ! My leave date is now definitely confirmed. I am leaving here May 7th, arriving home May 8th—possibly very late as it is a late boat that day, I think. That's terrific, isn't it ! I'm thrilled to have so early a prospect of seeing you all again. And Yorkshire and Linton should be lovely then. And it includes Whit. Just think—only 12 days hence ! And the date is quite definite unless leave is suspended again, or something else very untoward happens ! "

But it did happen and leave never matured. Jerry showed signs of life at last and the longed-for action resulted. The British Army moved up towards the Belgian frontier, but Geoffrey's last letter from France could tell us nothing of those terrific days. " Somewhere in ? Just a line to let you know that all's well. Life is very hectic, but equally interesting and exceptionally busy. There is always about four times as much to do as one can do in 24 hours, and so you just have to do all you can do and sleep in the odd moments when you are not doing it. I have at last got to the stage when sleep is far more important than eating, and if it's ever a case of a meal or half an hour's sleep the latter has it.

" This will be a poor letter. I can tell you nothing whatever of my activities—not even how I spend my time. But I am very well, fairly comfortable (at times) and having a terrific experience. There will be masses to tell you when I am home again, but I am afraid it must all wait until then. Sufficient to say that my days are very full and very interesting. I am very brown with continually being out in the open air in the open car. Hitler has struck an amazing patch of weather for this attack—continuous sun and blue skies for the past 14 days. I am longing to be able to get home again and tell you all about it. You know, in spite of everything, this is an amazing and invaluable experience for me and in certain ways will be of immense value in later life. I had better stop—things are beginning to happen again. I'll be home for Xmas!"

Geoff's letters ceased, but we knew from the papers what was happening. Germany was on the move and across the French and Belgian frontiers. The British troops advanced across the famous battlefields of the last war and towards Brussels with the French on their right and the Belgians on their left. But both flanks gave way and the retreat to the Dunkirk perimeter began. No need here to tell Geoff's verbal story of that retreat, described so many times before, but two or three personal incidents may be recalled."

The first is contained in a letter written at a much later date by one of Geoffrey's non-commissioned officers, Cpl. Prout, who later joined the same Commando troop as Geoffrey, was commissioned, and finished the war as a major : " Just before Dunkirk, we had arrived at Armentières, having been bombed and hounded by the Hun for days. We were all tired and hungry, and our first job was to get the men a square meal. Geoffrey stayed to see them started, and then went off after remarking to me, ' Proutie, I'm off to attempt to cope with an appetite that is already becoming famous in the British Army !'

"Almost immediately the Hun came over and savagely bombed the town for half an hour. We had few casualties, but the French suffered badly. Geoffrey appeared during the raid and shouted to me to get a lorry and a dozen men, after making sure that our own men were all right. The town was a pretty grim sight as we drove through it to a house that had been badly hit. Geoffrey had heard that a woman and children were buried in a cellar and that the French had given up hope of getting them out. Without hesitation he led his men into the ruined house, and there, among falling timber from the burning roof, and inspired by his determination and almost superhuman energy, we hacked our way through the debris to the cellar. The Military Police ordered us out but Geoffrey affected not to hear, knowing that the men would take no orders except from him. We heard a pathetic knocking on the other side of the cellar wall, and redoubled our efforts, but unfortunately by the time we had made an opening the knocking had ceased and the very strong smell of gas told its own sad story.

" We never had our dinner that night, but not a man regretted missing it."

Towards the end and near the perimeter, when all maps of the enemy's whereabouts were useless and every officer had to make his own decisions, Geoff was sent to meet ten lorries at a certain bridge and bring them back to the perimeter. When Geoff arrived he found only eight of the ten lorries there and the bridge was under heavy shell fire. He immediately directed the eight lorries back towards Dunkirk. Then he got into the ditch and considered what to do. Would the lorries ever find their way without him ? Should he follow them ? But if he did wouldn't people say he was afraid of the shell fire ? Suppose the other two lorries turned up and had no one to tell them where to go ? He turned to God and prayed for direction. " Follow those eight lorries at once " came clearly and insistently to him. He got into his car and went after them. When he caught up with them they had missed the road and were heading straight for the German lines. He heard later that the other two lorries never went to the bridge, they were diverted by other orders, and the bridge itself was blown up half an hour after Geoffrey left it. He told us this story as an illustration of how through all those terribly confused days never once had he found that God failed to give him direct instructions. It was an experience which he found valid through all his later adventures.

Arrived at his appointed spot within the perimeter, he reported to his Commanding Officer who told him now that he had got his ammunition through, to take his cars and lorries to a canal, destroy them with fire and pick axe, and throw them into the canal. The Commanding Officer later, with some amusement, recounted to Geoff that he seemed dazed by the order, that his jaw dropped, his eyes opened wide with horror and, forgetting military discipline, he ejaculated " What ! *me* destroy *my* cars, *my* lorries ! " On these vehicles Geoff had laboured, through days and nights of the long rigours of winter and the rains of the spring, to keep them in the pink of perfection on the road. The shock of the order was to him as to a father told to ill-treat his children.

Geoff brought all his men safely into Dunkirk where they waited amid the sand dunes for their turn for embarkation whilst Jerry bombed them from above. He told—at a later date—how, crouched alone in one of these sand holes he was sent suddenly sprawling by something hitting him hard in the middle of the back. As he lay, his mouth full of sand, thinking " Well, this is it—they've got me "—a voice sounded in his ear—" I say, I ff-feel a bb-bloody coward, how about you ? " This startling encounter was Geoff's first meeting with Captain Gustavus March-Phillipps, later destined to become his commanding officer, and who, as " Gus," with his characteristic slight stammer, was to become one of his closest friends. The turn for embarkation of Geoffrey and his Company did not come until towards the end. Under heavy shelling from the Germans they waited on the beach north of Dunkirk for a boat to take them off, whilst the enemy fire took its toll.

Geoffrey returned on a destroyer on which all night long through the journey surgeons were operating upon the wounded. The ship and her gallant company returned the next day for the remnants of the Forces still at Dunkirk, but alas, she was sunk on her return journey.

Like every other family whose men were there his family racked with anxiety waited for news. Never in the writer's experience did the telephone bring such joy as came towards the end of that evacuation. "Geoffrey—speaking from Dover—just landed from a destroyer—entraining for Tenby, South Wales—can you meet me there?" We could—within an hour or two we were away and there followed the happiest reunion this family has ever known. Geoff told how they were repeatedly bombed at sea, of the heroism of the amateur crews of the little boats, the merchant sailors and the naval men who worked the Dunkirk miracle; of the generosity of the people of Dover, Kent, and right across southern England who met the famished trainloads of men with tea and food and fruit at every station; of the decorations along the route as though the Great Retreat were a Glorious Victory!

Indeed, England rightly celebrated and thanked God for the Great Deliverance and with immeasurable relief welcomed home her sons and girded her loins inspired by her great Prime Minister to fight on the beaches and in the villages and towns—if need be—for her freedom.

A few days later Geoff was back at Aldershot helping to re-form his Corps. His first letter from there caused some dismay. "We are going overseas shortly. Apparently, of the four Corps H.Q.s that were in the last B.E.F. we are the only one at present going out again and we are going out not as II Corps H.Q., but as the G.H.Q. of the British Forces in France. Fun and games! Meanwhile, life is frantically busy. I cannot imagine how we can sail on Thursday, although by then we expect to be fully re-equipped with new transport."

Then six days later came further news. "Well, we've been to Southampton, loaded three-quarters of our transport into ships, unloaded it again, and returned back here. I don't know what it all means or what happens next, nor does anyone in this H.Q. Apparently British troops are leaving France as fast as they can be shipped and so it looks as though we are evacuating

France and she is going to accept ' terms.' Anyway, it's all pretty depressing. I imagine that we shall concentrate all our efforts on Home Defence and probably become II Corps H.Q. again in a similar formation to our B.E.F. job. A pity—I'd much sooner be fighting overseas. There you do at least feel you are doing something to keep the ' wolf from the door ' so to speak, but to form up in England and wait for him to come means that this country of ours will be turned into a battlefield. Still, I suppose it will at least have the advantage of making certain people in England know that we *are* at war, and realise what invasion really does mean. And we really shall feel that we are fighting to protect English soil. Anyway, above all things, I do hope that we don't make any kind of treaty—even though France does pack up. We would never be able to hold our heads up again."

CHAPTER III

COMMANDO—ON SPECIAL SERVICE

GEOFF BEGAN TO get very restive in his job, in its paper work and lack of activity. In the autumn a letter arrived telling of a decision which changed his whole career. " I have the biggest news that you have heard from me for some time ! Do you remember, Dad, at Tenby we were discussing the ' Ironsides.' Well, since yesterday morning things have been working very quickly here, and I have volunteered for, and been accepted as a ' Commando.' From the attached notes you will see what that means. In short, it means that I am a member of a Force that can be sent anywhere at a moment's notice to do any sort of a defensive, counter-attacking or raiding job.

" Of course, it's absolutely terrific—it's the grandest job in the Army that one could possibly get, and is a job that if properly carried out can be of enormous value. Just think of operating under direct orders from the C. in C. ! No red tabs, no paper work, none of all the things that are so cramping and infuriating and disheartening that there are in the Army. Just pure operations, the success of which depends principally on

----

THE SPORT OF THE SNOW

PLATE Va

Just before the start of the Oxford-Cambridge 'Varsity Ski-race, 1937, on Geoff's Twenty-first Birthday, the Slalom being won by him for Cambridge that day

PLATE Vb

Geoff's first Ski-climb (aged nine), and his sister

PLATE Vc

Geoff after winning the oldest and best known British Downhill Ski-race—the " Roberts of Kandahar "—in a blinding snowstorm, at Wengen, 1938-9

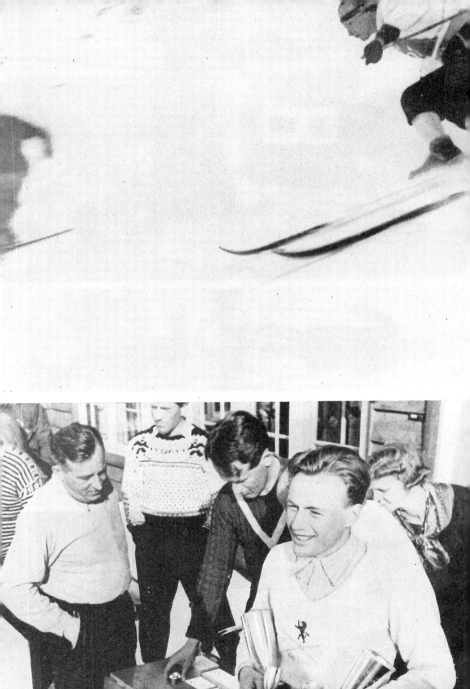

oneself and the men one has oneself picked to do the job with you. It's terrific ! It's revolutionary, and one can hardly imagine it ever happening in this old Army of ours, but I am convinced that the Commandos can be of very real value in ensuring ultimate victory in this war. It is a very similar thing to what we heard of the Ironsides (which don't seem to have materialised), a mobile fighting unit that can get anywhere in the shortest possible time to do a job. Well, what do you think of it ? Do write and tell me all your views soon. I, in my own mind, have considered it very carefully, and I know that I have taken the right decision.

" The job I am doing here does not need any special engineering or automobile ability, whereas I do feel that I have qualifications as a Commando and that I have the right temperament. Ski-ing was apparently a great pull with the War Office in my favour, as was the Cambridge University Hawks Club membership, and rowing record. Also I'm as fit as most people, and finally, I'll have my heart in the work with the knowledge that I am in the right job. I am in ' B ' Troop, No. 7 Commando. Lt.-Col. Lister, M.C., of the Buffs, is O.C. of my Commando. O.C. of the Troop is my friend Gus March-Phillipps (Capt.) R.A., and the other subaltern is my very good friend, John Colbeck of the Tank Corps. The ' Troop ' consists of a Captain in command, and two subalterns each in charge of one of

----

PLATE VIa

Racing in Norway

Geoffrey descended an altitude difference of 2,000 feet in 1 minute 33.1 seconds, entailing a speed at times of over sixty miles per hour, and tied for first place with the Norwegian champion

---

PLATE VIb

Anglo-Norwegian Champion, 1938

Geoffrey as English captain accepts the Team's Trophy and his own Challenge Cup

D

the two sections. Each section has 23 men and so the whole strength of the Troop is 50 men. Thus I shall be in command of 23 *picked* men—all volunteers. We have about 200 men (volunteers) from which to pick the 47 for our troop. *Everything* depends on the men we choose. We ourselves select the men and have the right to take from the lists of volunteers any we like, so you see we have a very free hand. It is rather frightening, this selection of the men. This thing can either be a flop or a colossal success, and so much depends on the men— they must be utterly reliable, steady and intelligent. But with the right men what a wonderful fellowship we can have in the unit—just picture it—a command of 23 of my own picked men. I can know every man personally, the sort of job he can do, his good points and his weak ones.

" On parade and on a job there must be rigid discipline. Off parade there will be a great fellowship. At all times there must be absolute trust and confidence.

" There will be no punishments—a man is either IN or OUT. If he is in, he is a 100 per cent. in—if not, he will be out as there are far more volunteers than opportunities at present. There will be no paper work, no administrative work. No billeting problems, no feeding problems as we feed and billet ourselves. Every man gets 6/8 a day above his normal pay for this purpose, every officer gets 13/4 a day extra.

" Well, don't you agree with me now that it's a real job ? I can't imagine a better.

" One of our first objects is to get really fit ! Think of it—training again ! I've been longing to do that for months ! Cross-country runs, P.T., up early, riding in the mornings (by the way I've been out 6 to 8 a.m. for the last seven mornings now), getting really fit is to be one of the first objects for all. Then map-reading, night patrol and compass work in unknown country by night will all come into the training which is going to be very strenuous. Think of it—a job that is operational instead of purely paper work !

" This is how I got into it—March-Phillipps (he has just got an M.B.E. in France) was selected by Col. Lister (the O.C.) as ' B ' Troop Leader. He was told he could have a free hand in picking two volunteer subalterns from the whole of the Southern Command (about 30 volunteered) for his two section leaders. Colbeck (Royal Tank Corps) had volunteered and was immediately picked and after interviews by the War Office was selected. Until then I had not heard anything about this at all, and then I heard March-Phillipps discussing it and knew it was the thing for me. I know him very well and after he knew I wanted to volunteer he accepted me as the other subaltern immediately. The proposal went up to Col. Lister together with my ' on paper ' qualifications and March-Phillipps's strong recommendation. Col. Lister accepted it and approached the War Office, they communicated with Brig. Gale of this H.Q. who apparently ' did his stuff by me,' and yesterday evening the War Office wired that I was appointed ! This all happened in about twenty-four hours, and now I am only waiting for the official written confirmation to come through—perhaps a day or two— a relief to come to take over my job here, and then we can start interviewing the volunteers and picking our men.

" Colbeck is a great friend of mine. We have seen a lot of each other since the H.Q. re-formed over this side. He was over in France but was at Advance H.Q. whereas I was at Rear H.Q. March-Phillipps, too, is one of the people here with whom I get on best, and so all knowing each other so well, we should work well together and be a good team.

" By the way, my engineering was a good pull as regards my qualifications for the job. I expect I shall again be made responsible for our transport and machinery and so will still be partly on the same line !

" Incidentally, this means immediate promotion to Lieutenant, and I expect to put my second pip up as soon as the official confirmation is through.

"I expect to be sent home on a short leave (48 hours) in the very near future, before I take up the new job in fact, as I haven't yet really had the 48 hours at home ex B.E.F. leave to which we are all entitled, and there is quite a push in certain quarters here to getting me that. So here's hoping to see you all soon!

"By the way, Jimmy is coming with me. As soon as he heard I was on the job he announced his intention of coming too. And I'll be mighty glad to have him as a right hand man!

"Well, let me know soon your reactions to all this. It will be a surprise, I know. But don't worry. I'm convinced that it's the job for me and I know I have taken the right decision. And what else really matters?"

In a letter dated 1/8/40 headed "B" Troop, No. 7 Commando, he describes the training and cultivation of the *esprit de corps* of the earliest commandos. "This life is absolutely terrific. There is something about the fellowship and hardship and toughness of it that appeals to me enormously. There is so much to tell you about it that I can't start to tell you in a letter and so will have to wait·until the week-end. Sufficient to say that there is such a tremendous spirit of keenness, smartness and discipline in the Troop, that I know these Commando units really are going to mean something. I believe that through the spirit of Commando units an entirely new spirit can be created in the Army, and will be created. We have got a grand crowd of chaps, keen as mustard, exceptionally fit physically, and very alert mentally. We took a lot of trouble selecting them. We are the first troop of No. 7 Commando (Col. Lister) to report that we are formed and in training (there are 10 Troops each of 50 men in the Commando) so that is a feather in our caps, or rather in M-P's cap as he did all the pioneer work. And we will always remain the first Troop! M-P is a very stout fellow—we have a great deal in common. He is a keen naturalist, a great lover of the open air, of country places, and, above all, of this England of ours and all its unique beauty and life.

This will interest you—he was at Ampleforth ! (He is now thirty-two so was before my time at Bootham). Incidentally, also, he is the first Army officer I have met so far who kneels down by the side of his bed for ten minutes before he goes to sleep. M-P is a great worshipper and disciple of the Knights of Old, believes that the spirit of Drake and Raleigh, of Robert the Bruce and of Oliver Cromwell is the spirit that will save England to-day and give her a name that the world will once again look up to. And I'm sure he's right. It isn't a spirit of Safety First, but it's a spirit of adventure, of giving instead of getting, of clean living and physical fitness, of comradeship and unity, and, above all, it's God's spirit. Of that I'm sure. Don't you see what this show can mean ?

" You will want to know how we are living. We are all (the whole Troop) in a large house in Newmarket, and the Provost Company (to whom we are temporarily attached for pay, rations, etc.) has lent us two cooks. John and I share one room, M-P has a room to himself, the sergeants have a room, the men are about eight in a room. The house is entirely unfurnished except for tables and benches that we have got together. There is a bathroom and lavatory with running water. We three officers eat exactly the same food as the men, but in a different room. And it is very good.

" Our transport consists of M-P's car (a terrific 30–98 Velox ! !), two motor cycles and a 30-cwt. lorry. But we don't use it much. When we want to go anywhere, we walk, as our primary object is to get as tough as possible. When we finally move from here to a new location on the coast, we shall walk—60 or 70 miles—in two or three days, bivouacking at nights in barns and haylofts and living on our ration allowance of 6/8 a day.

" To-day's programme has been typical. Reveille 6-30, training run 7 (about a mile) followed by P.T., breakfast 8, parade 9, inspection, route march 8-10 miles (with arms, in battle dress, belts, etc.) at fast pace, including cross-country work, map reading, compass work, moving through cover, etc. Lunch 1, swimming parade 2-30 for 1½ hours' swimming, running, exercising, etc. Tea at 4-30. Lecture by M-P for three-quarters of an hour at 5. Free for the evening at 6. A fairly full day, and hard work, but makes one feel grand, even though a little stiff! Later on, of course, there will be weapon training, range practice, cross-country runs, hare and hounds, treasure hunts, mock operations, night operations, etc. The training programme can and will be made very fascinating. I have heaps more to tell you all about this when I get home at the week-end, but meanwhile must cut things short.

" By the way, I have two pips up now. Going round the battalions and units in 18 Division selecting our men from those that had volunteered was hard work, but great fun. After asking endless questions of candidates all day long at one point I caught M-P asking a fellow ' Can you marry ? Are you swim ? ' !!! "

Before the end of the year they had moved to secret training quarters on an island off the West Coast of Scotland. The seriousness of their dedication to their new duties is very evident in a letter home dated 12/12/40.

" It was topping to hear from you again to-day for the first time since my leave, as I have just got the letter you sent dated 7/12/40. Your wishes of Godspeed and good luck will be always a great strength to me and a source of great power to know that all of you at home are with me in spirit, and are putting up a barrage of prayer for me. Don't pray for my safety or for my speedy return, but pray that I am alive to my responsibilities, courageous in danger, and that I have the strength to do my bit of a job to the utmost. Remember, I am responsible for 25 men—I mustn't let them down. Pray too that I am continually sensitive to the real ' Commander-in-Chief' for then I can have continual guidance and my ' lines of communication ' can never be cut !

"And I too shall continually be thinking and praying for you all at home. You will always be in my thoughts, and especially at Christmas time shall I be at home in every way except physically. May it be a very, very happy Christmas for you all, and as jolly a one as war conditions will allow. The next best thing to being there myself will be hearing all about it in your letters. My very dear love, Geoffrey."

A letter written two days before Christmas 1940 reveals how thus early and at their own expense the Troop were training themselves for water-borne raids on enemy coasts. Does this mark one of the earliest ideas of Combined Operations, later to become so famous ?

" We came here by the boat last Saturday (21st) as I told you in my letter of the 20th, and are doomed to be in solitary confinement because we ' know too much ' to be allowed loose. This is certainly going to be a ' memorable ' Christmas, but memorable because of its apparent lack of ' merriment and what-not.' Actually, we shall manage to have quite a lot of fun. We are on an island, a tiny little place, with hardly any form of life whatsoever, but very picturesque and very lovely. There is no sort of amusement whatever for the troops, though, and there is not a pub within eight miles.

" We are living in a hotel which is only open in summer and is utterly unfurnished and empty except for tables and chairs. There is no heating, but most rooms have fireplaces in which we burn vast quantities of wood. No lighting either, except candles and small oil lamps that we have bought. Running water here and there but only cold ! Actually billets in houses had been arranged for the seven of us (all the other officers have gone into billets) but we thought it would be more fun to live with our troops and would also cheer them up over Christmas and prevent them feeling that they hadn't had a very square deal. Gus and Colin are, of course, two of the seven. Actually we have a lot of fun —we have to do all our own buying and cooking of food and do everything in just the one room—eating, sleeping, cooking and living. Rather a shambles. The men also look after themselves similarly and are between 5 and 20 in the different rooms all over the hotel.

' Scrounging ' and making up bits of furniture, cooking utensils, crockery, cutlery, etc., exercises one's ingenuity to the utmost. It is at times like this that Jimmy really proves his worth—he really is a brick and worth any three other batmen.

" Until to-night I have had no bedding except for six blankets and sleeping on the bare boards with two blankets beneath and four on top and a coat for a pillow isn't too comfortable in the middle of winter, but to-night my valise has arrived and so I shall sleep on my camp bed and should keep warm.

" Colin is proving to fit in with M-P and me extremely well. I like him immensely. Jolly good cook, too, which may partly explain our enthusiasm for him. But I am just beginning to wonder if I didn't eat rather too much of his excellent Welsh rarebit for supper.

"And now for some real news—we have all clubbed together (putting in between £1 and 10/- each man) and have bought—guess what—a boat ! She is $5\frac{1}{2}$ tons, yawl rigged, 32 feet long by $9\frac{1}{2}$ beam and has a 15 h.p. (auxiliary) paraffin engine. Her name is *I'm Alone* and we bought her here from an ex-fisherman of this village who is now in the Navy, for £35—a very good bargain. Her general condition is excellent, but she needs a certain amount doing before we use her. For the small capital outlay per person that she has meant we are going to get a lot of fun out of her. We hope to teach the men how to sail, navigate, use a compass and run an engine, and, generally be ' handy ' with a boat. But apart from that, it is an excellent thing to have her, as it gives the men a new interest—partly due to delay and postponement, and partly due to our training the men were going very stale. This ship has really made them enthusiastic and given them a real interest. Also it is a job of work to keep all really busy over Christmas when there will be nothing whatever to do. When we leave here we hope to be able to get her over to Girvan where some friends of M-P's will look after her, until we return to this district again, as this part of the world is likely to be our base. As you know, Gus is an experienced yachtsman and so is the ' skipper,' whilst I have been appointed ' first mate ' !

" We have been working on her all day yesterday and to-day—caulking seams, cutting, trimming and fitting a new mast, decking, making a second cabin out of the fish-hold, rigging up electric light, overhauling the engine, painting, splicing ropes, etc., and every man has his own job to do. They are all as happy as could be and we hope to be ready to put to sea on Christmas Day ! She is said to be a wonderful sea boat and very fast withal. Two of the men are living on her now as she rides at anchor out in the loch. After the war (!) Gus and I will probably buy out the men's shares in the boat and have her ourselves. We are already planning our voyages !

"Apart from the ship (work on which is officially approved as ' training ' for the time we are here) other training consists mainly of physical exercise.

" The weather is mild so far for the time of year, although some days the wind is very bitter, but very little rain.

" What magnificent hills ! Of course, before we never really saw them, but they are the most impressive and jagged peaks I have ever seen in Britain, more so even than Skye. I shall be getting up some soon. Most of the snow has now gone.

" We are getting quite a Christmassy spirit in our room as we have Christmas cards spread across the mantelpiece, and to-morrow will be getting some holly to decorate the walls. I am thinking of you all continually and wishing you the very happiest of Christmasses. And now it is past midnight and all is silent in the room except for the snores of my companions and the crackle of a few dying embers in the grate. Good night all ! Very much love, Geoff."

On New Year's Eve he again enthuses over the boat. " The *I'm Alone* really has been a grand investment. We spent about six days working on her from stem to stern and then got to sea for the first time on the 28th. A pouring wet day with high winds, and quite a sea. It was enormous fun—she is a magnificent dirty weather craft, but a bit slow and heavy in light breezes. We were soaked through all day, and took many a wave right over the bows and decks, but she never showed a sign of misbehaviour and shook herself straight out of everything. It was a real test for the mast, and it stood its test wonderfully. You will remember we completely made the mast ourselves from what a week ago was a pine tree ! To-day we have again been at sea all day in mild breezes and have been teaching the troop to sail, map read, navigate, use compasses, etc. To-morrow we are using her for a scheme embodying landing, etc. She is a marvellous craft.

" That seems to be about all. Only 1½ hours left of 1940 so I'll wish you the best of days for 1941. May it see a reunited family again before the year is over and the war a thing of the past. Good night, and God bless ! Geoffrey."

Strenuous training followed, in long treks over the Highlands, with no equipment except such as was carried on the back, no arranged commissariat, sleeping in the ditches or under the lee of walls for nights on end during which it usually rained.

Then followed a long period without letters or news of any kind, except that Geoff hinted he might be engaged on duties having some resemblance to those of the "Scarlet Pimpernel," but we were left guessing. It subsequently transpired that Geoff had embarked on a submarine—the *Tigris*—Commander H. F. Bone, D.S.O. and Bar, D.S.C.—and been away on a long sea trip in which, of course, operational silence was observed. One of the objects of the voyage was to put Geoffrey and André Desgrange—a Free Frenchman in his commando—down on the coast of the Bay of Biscay and there make contact, at an agreed rendezvous south of the Loire estuary, with two Secret Service agents who had been operating in France and bring them back to

England.   Geoffrey and André were to land, each in a separate collapsible rubber canoe of the sporting Folbot type—one of the first occasions on which this device had been applied to such work.

The submarine surfaced in the dark of the night at the appointed time and place, two or three miles off shore, the Folbots were placed on the deck and manned and floated off. All went well until the shore, a sandy beach, was reached, but an unlucky rock tore a hole in the Frenchman's boat and rendered it useless for the return. The two crawled up and down the beach to find the signal light which would be given by the " agents " whom they were to pick up, but no light was seen and under strict orders they had to give up the search that night in order to get back to the submarine before moonrise to enable it to get away unobserved.

Arrangements had been made that, if the agents were not found the first night, an attempt should be made a few nights later, if conditions permitted. The submarine again took up its position two or three miles off shore and surfaced. Unfortunately a very heavy sea was running. Observation was kept on the shore and Geoffrey thought he saw a signal light, but it was not repeated. The Commander of the submarine had not seen it and tried to discourage Geoffrey from attempting to land on account of the heavy sea and the flimsy nature of the portable Folbot rubber canoe in which the attempt would have to be made. He further stated that the submarine must leave at 3 a.m. on account of moonrise and was emphatic he could not endanger his ship by remaining longer.

Geoffrey had an inward assurance that the agents were at the appointed place and that he must try to go and bring them off. His request that he should be allowed to make the attempt was finally agreed by the Commander.

The two remaining canoes were got out on deck with the intention that Geoffrey and André Desgrange should take one each in order to bring back the two agents.

Misfortune in the shape of a particularly heavy wave swept one of the canoes away. Geoffrey perforce had to go alone. Time and again the attempt was made to launch him in the canoe but each time the swell upset the frail boat and threw Geoffrey into the water—it was the middle of winter. At last in a temporary lull the attempt succeeded and he managed to paddle to the shore three miles away. He scouted up and down the beach but saw no signal light. Finally as time drew short he abandoned caution and ran up and down the coast shouting and flashing his torch. At the very last available moment his signal was answered and the two agents located. It transpired that they had been unable to signal on the previous occasion, or earlier that night, because they also had under observation the German coast watchers and these had only just left that position.

The three crawled back to the hidden canoe unobserved. Geoff told the two " agents " that if they cared to risk the journey he would take them both at once, as he could not come back a second time for the *Tigris* had to leave before moonrise. He warned them the Folbot canoe was only built to carry two, and that a heavy sea was running, and that the submarine was two or three miles away. They elected to take the risk and after an adventurous journey in which the high swell constantly threatened the heavily laden flimsy craft, by constant bailing and hard paddling, they managed to reach the submarine exactly at 3 a.m. as she was submerging and preparing to leave. When taken aboard Geoff found he had been given up and that the Royal Navy officers had gone so far towards a compliment as to remark " Poor old Apple, he wasn't such a bad sort for an Army man ! "

A few days later on the homeward run, he considered himself fortunate in being present in a naval action. The *Tigris* submarine located a 10,000 ton enemy oil tanker in the Bay. Being towards the end of her cruise her store of torpedoes was almost exhausted, and owing to the heavy sea she failed to make a hit at the usual range. Commander Bone decided to surface and fight it out with his single light gun against the enemy's heavier guns, although one hit on the *Tigris* would have sunk her. In the words of the song, Geoff helped to " pass the ammunition." A long and exciting artillery duel ensued in a running fight lasting an hour and a half, in which Commander Bone added to his already brilliant career the distinction of crippling the 10,000 tonner and knocking out her guns by his own lighter gunfire, after which he came in to short range and sank her with a torpedo. She blew up with a great explosion which, at that short distance, violently shook the submarine. An alarm clock fell from its support on André's head. At that moment, an officer on the conning tower shouted down " We've got her." André, rubbing his head ruefully, remarked " Oui, et moi aussi ! " Geoff always regarded the fight as one of his greatest thrills and vowed if ever he served in the Navy he hoped it would be in the Submarine Service.

Some time later, on Geoff's return from one of his sailings in the Channel, he had a pleasant surprise in regard to these French landings, for the *London Gazette* of 23/5/41 had the announcement :—

War Office.
23rd May, 1941.

The King has been graciously pleased to approve the undermentioned award in recognition of gallant and distinguished services in the field :—

The Military Cross.

Lieutenant (acting Captain) John Geoffrey Appleyard (86639), *Royal Army Service Corps.*

Geoffrey wrote : " Thank you so very much for your telegrams—it was grand of you to send them. But what an amazing surprise ! I hadn't the foggiest idea there was anything in the wind whatsoever ! We came into port yesterday afternoon about 4 after a hard eight hours at sea and someone came on board and handed me three telegrams—two greetings ones. As I was not in the midst of a birthday I thought people must think I had just got engaged or married or something! Then I opened them and found they were of a congratulatory nature and was still baffled until I suddenly saw how they were addressed! But how did you know? I suppose it must have been in the *Gazette* or something, but I haven't seen a paper.

" With your wire was one from ' the Brigadier and the boys at H.Q.' and many others.

" It was such an extraordinary surprise that I haven't quite got used to it yet. It all goes to show that the Army at present must be pretty hard up for people to give medals to! There had been no whisper of it at all when I was up in London, so it came as an absolute shock!

" Gus, Tim and I had a night ashore to celebrate. We went to a flick and then had dinner and spent the night ashore, returning here at 10-30 this morning, Sunday. Since then we have been at sea all day. We dropped anchor here again at 8-30 p.m. and it has been a terrific, rip-roaring day. There has been three parts of a gale of wind and torrential rain, so we have had a glorious day of immensely hard work. I am physically quite tired out now, with hands swollen and sore from ropes and water.

" You would get my telegram last night saying I am getting a few days' leave to celebrate at home? "

Having now had experience of action on land and sea Geoffrey thought it necessary for the raiding jobs he had in mind to gain experience in the air in order that he could, when necessary, lead troops on airborne expeditions which, although they had not at that early date been carried out, were under discussion. He went to Ringway Aerodrome, Cheshire, for this purpose, and later wrote : " I got back from Ringway late last night (by road). We left there at 3 p.m. and had to come round by Hertford. I have had an extremely busy week. We were up at 5-30 a.m. yesterday, had two parachute jumps before breakfast, did a hard day's work till 3 and then left for London. I didn't get a bite of food or a drink of any sort from breakfast at 9 a.m. until we got to Hertford at 8 p.m. There just wasn't a minute to spare for it. One of our majors was with me.

" It was fun and novel being on an aerodrome. I managed to get occasional flights in ' Whitleys ' when they were on test, etc. They are incredible planes, steady as liners, and you hardly have any sensation of flying. The most interesting flight was once testing the plane on single-engine flying, and I sat in the front gunner (and bomb aimer) position, which is right in the very tip of the nose (in front of the propellers) and is like being in a glass ball suspended in the sky as all the walls and floor beneath one's feet are transparent. Fascinating.

" For many years I have had a great desire to know what a parachute jump felt like, and whilst at Ringway I managed to persuade the powers that be to let me try and do the full course in the time. Jumping was not the reason I went up there, but it fitted in very well. As well as the actual jumps there is a lot of ground training to do,. packing chutes, landing exercises, etc., but we just managed to squeeze it in, even though to finish off it did mean two jumps before brekker on our last day ! We were badly held up by wind though on some days, making jumping impossible.

" It's a remarkable business, but I don't think any-one would pretend that actually leaving the plane is enjoyable. I was very frightened each time, but not so much as I have often been before a ski-race. But it seems such an unnatural thing to do, to drop out into space, and all your natural instincts revolt at the idea. The period after the 'chute opens, though, really is enjoyable—the most glorious feeling of suspension and floating in mid-air. But you can't enjoy it long before you begin to get really worried about the rate the ground is coming up. You hit pretty hard and if you are unlucky or unskilful, or both, can get hurt. I had an accident on my first jump as I got a nasty gust of wind a split second before landing and landed hard straight on the base of my spine and back of my head ! ! —or so they tell me. I suffered from complete amnesia (is that the word for loss of memory ?). Most remarkable. I was fully conscious and in full control of all my physical movements (so I'm told—I don't remember anything about it) but had no memory whatever. I knew my name, but nothing else—didn't know where I was, whom I knew there, what I was doing, or even that I had just done a parachute drop! After about three hours I completely recovered (except for a headache), but still to this day have no memory of a period of about three-quarters of an hour from the second before I hit the ground until being in a car returning to the aerodrome. Although in the meantime they tell me I had behaved quite normally, rolled up my 'chute, walked about half a mile to a hut, where I packed the 'chute away and did various other things, and heard a criticism of my drop ! ! Moreover, on returning to the same place, hut, etc., next day, it awoke no chord of memory ! I have felt no ill effects since at all.

"All my other landings were ' happy ones,' and I was on my feet each time and in control of the 'chute within a few seconds of hitting the ground.

" You always have to pack your own 'chute before a drop—with an R.A.F. parachute man watching and checking you. It is an easier process than one would

----

PLATE VIIa
England's Captain shakes hands with Norway's Manager

PLATE VIIb
Geoffrey—a member of the Cambridge ice-hockey "Eskimos"

PLATE VIIc
On the Norwegian Tour

imagine though, and is really a matter of just being absolutely certain that certain things are done in the right sequence and manner.

"With this method of dropping, a properly packed parachute is practically bound to open and there is really no chance at all of it not doing so. It's all very fascinating and interesting, but, although I have, on the general outlook, greatly enjoyed doing the jumping, I have no wish to do any more until or unless I have to.

"By the way, the parachuting is no longer secret as you may have gathered. I am now qualified for and wearing ' parachute wings ' on the arm of my uniform. It's rather a nice badge and has been authorised in Army Council Orders.

"I think I had better stop. I've lots more to tell you but I am so very tired and it's nearly midnight. By the way, the Brigadier intends to do some drops when he is next in the North ! Rather grand, don't you think ? He is a wonderful man—we all think the world of him."

During the spring of 1941, Captain Gustavus March-Phillipps, M.B.E., with Geoffrey as second in command, were permitted to select from their Commandos and elsewhere a small group of hand-picked men to form a Special Service Unit, and were instructed to train for amphibious duties, and work out schemes for raiding the enemy, subject to the approval of the Special Service Department of the War Office, and of the Admiralty.

To their great delight their suggestion to be allotted a Brixham trawler for the purpose of training and subsequent raids was accepted by the War Office. They suggested such would be ideal as, being of wood, it would not affect magnetic mines and, being primarily a sailing ship—with only an auxiliary engine—it could be used for night raiding without drawing enemy attention.

PLATE VIII

Water Ski-ing at Scarborough

Reproduced by arrangement with Fox Photos Ltd.

The acquisition of a ship for their purpose is described by Prout as follows :—

" Having obtained agreement in principle to the proposal of small scale raids Gus pulled off a feat that only he could have got away with. Although having no authority to proceed he calmly requisitioned a Brixham trawler whose attractive name was *Maid Honor*. With her he secured her Skipper, Blake Glanville, and sailed her from Brixham to Poole ! At Poole Bar ' Franco,' Senior Trinity House Pilot, was tossing about in a heavy swell waiting for a deep sea trawler, long overdue. Franco was disgusted, cold and miserable when a Brixham trawler arrived under sail, and he brusquely demanded whether this —— hooker had an engine, and if so, to start the censored thing and get on in. Gus nearly had apoplexy at the description of the ' Maid ' as a ' hooker,' and a wordy battle followed in which the Pilot added fuel to the fire by remarks in very nautical language about ' Yachts.' Gus won in the end by offering the Pilot a cup of tea, and the thought of anyone drinking *tea* on a day like that so offended that worthy salt that he was speechless ! Thus began a real and lasting friendship with a very great character.

" Berthed in Poole, Gus informed an astonished Navy of the requisition, who in turn informed an astonished Brigadier, who won the everlasting gratitude of the crew by backing us up through thick and thin. Shore headquarters were established at the old Antelope Hotel, where ' Pop ' treated us with much kindness over our many exorbitant demands. ' Pop ' remains to-day a very great friend of all who served under Gus and Apple, and the Antelope is our natural rendezvous for re-unions."

Maid Honor's sails were reddish brown—she was a beautiful ship and became a source of great joy to her gallant company. She had sleeping accommodation for five to eight persons. Geoff's boyhood friend and Linton neighbour, Graham Hayes, of the Borderers, was invited to join them. Receiving permission from his C.O., he eagerly did so and brought to their aid his great experience as a sailor, as before the war he went round the world ' before the mast ' in the *Pommern*, a Finnish owned sailing ship on the grain run from Australia.

Prout continues : " Very soon afterwards the rest of the crew began to arrive : first myself, then André Desgrange, a Free Frenchman whose inability to speak English had no effect on his instantaneous popularity ; then Andy Lassen, a Dane, later as Major Lassen to win a most brilliant but posthumous V.C. In due course, Buzz Perkins and Denis Tottenham arrived, and finally, remembering ' the cook of all cooks,' we succeeded in obtaining Ernest Evison, whose artistry so often made the fastidious Gus wax lyrical over food, and was responsible for sighs of utter satisfaction from Apple and Graham, whose appetites had to be seen to be believed !

"Always with us was the vast, rock-like and beloved figure of Skipper Blake Glanville. He fathered all of us, and taught us all we ever came to know in the handling of the *Maid*. We all owe a great debt of gratitude to Blake, for the success of his young pupils on the sea was very largely due to the thoroughness of his teaching. In the evenings he delighted the entire crew by spinning yarns of the Brixham Trawler Fleet—(' I only exaggerate a little, mind 'ee ! ')—and teaching us how to make ' Turk's Heads ' and ' Matthew Walkers.' On one occasion when sailing past Portland Bill, Gus had got off his course slightly and found no alternative but to sail through the renowned race. He hurriedly aroused Blake from the watch below. Blake weighed up the situation and remarked slowly, ' Well, well, just batten down the hatches, keep her on her course, and I'll go below and make 'ee all a cup of tea ! ' The ship got through with nothing worse than a lot of ' green ' over her, and Blake's tea restored confidence all round.

"At this time a battle was going on for the body of the last, but by no means the least, member of the

crew to join the *Maid*.   The C.O. of Britain's only
Parachute Battalion had no wish to part with Sgt.-Major
Tom Winter.   On the other hand, Graham, who had
come from that unit, was determined to get him, and to
our great good fortune, Gus's peculiar and unorthodox
methods prevailed at the War Office and Tom Winter
joined us officially in August 1941."

Their life was now spent in secret training for
amphibious operations aboard the *Maid* whose berth,
when at home, was a remote creek of Poole Harbour.
Geoffrey writes : " Still at Poole, as you see, and likely
to be here quite a while longer as there is much work
and training to be done.   However, we are learning a
lot and all continues to go very well.   Graham has
arrived—last Sunday to be exact—and is in great form.
He suits the job and the job suits him admirably, and
he fits in with the party very well.   Since he arrived he
and I have started having a swim early each morning—
at 6-45 (*i.e.*, 4-45 sun time !).   Cold, but refreshing,
and I need something pretty drastic to wake me up these
days because I sleep so soundly.

" We had a fine run back from Brixham, but rather
light winds.   Rather a noisy night at Weymouth (where
we put in) as a lot of bombs were dropped at intervals
all night.   Here at Poole, by all rights (touch wood) we
should be absolutely immune from bomb danger as we
are right out in the wilds, miles from anywhere, up a
creek.   It is very quiet and lonely, but very lovely.
Thousands of all kinds of waders and sea birds all
around—especially shelduck, herons, and curlews.
There is a big heronry nearby.

" One night, Gus and I sailed the dinghy five miles
up the river to Wareham, had a meal at the Black
Bear, and then sailed back again on the ebb in the late
evening.   It was a still, warm evening, and it was one
of the most lovely experiences I have ever had—just
' ghosting ' down in the twilight between great reed-
beds, sandbanks and mud flats with the lovely evening
light, and no sounds at all but the cries of warblers and

waders and the lapping and rustle of the water against the boat. It really was beautiful.

" Last Sunday, two of the crew and I landed on Arne peninsula (our nearest bit of land) and walked a mile over the heath to Arne village where we went to service in the tiny, very old church. A very simple and beautiful service—only three-quarters of an hour ! Afterwards I was approached by the ' lady ' of the village (apparently) who offered us the hospitality of her home, hot baths, etc., whenever we wanted one, so doubtless we shall avail ourselves of the offer soon.

" The weather has mostly been too good for us—hot and calm with a lot of sun. However, to-day there is half a gale of wind from the west and we have had a really hard day's sailing and training in handling the ship. We are really very happily placed—if it's fine and calm we can get on with the work on the ship in perfect conditions—if it's wild and stormy we also revel in it as it means some good sea sailing. In general, at present, our training for the day is just planned according to the weather the day brings forth. We are very busy at all hours of the day and night— but it's such grand work that one doesn't want any time off.

" Graham shot a duck two days ago, after a three-quarter hour stalk. It is for the.pot to-night ! He has a very good little .22 repeating rifle. We hope to get quite a lot of duck and rabbits with it as we get enormous appetites and our meat and other rations don't really satisfy them. We shall, of course, shoot only ' for the pot.'

" To-night the wind and the rain are lashing down on the ship and we feel very comfortable and snug here below with the ship firmly fastened to her mooring.

" Graham and I have just been chatting for an hour— about the Lake District, the Dales, Linton and other Yorkshire places, and now I feel quite homesick ! I'd like a breath of moorland air again. Funny thing— there are lots of curlews here, but although superficially

they are the same birds, they don't seem to have anything like the haunting call of 'the curlews faintly
crying 'mid the wastes of Cumberland.'

> *Ah ! to win them back and clamber*
> *Braced anew with winds I love.*

That was what Noel Oxland wrote in 'Outward
Bound.' Yes, like him, I'm looking forward to that !
Well, I must to bed."

To keep physically fit was a part of Geoffrey's
religion. " I am sitting on the deck just by the mizzen-
mast in nothing but a pair of swimming shorts. It is
another glorious day in this unbroken spell of cloudless
weather. Buzz (one of the crew) and I have just walked
back across the heath from Arne where we went to
morning service in the little old church.

" I had a marvellous afternoon yesterday—it was
one of the hottest days yet, and somehow really hot
weather seems to make me more energetic than usual.
So, as it was a free Saturday afternoon and we all had it
off, I decided to go for a cross-country run, when
everyone else decided to go to sleep. I went ashore on
Arne peninsula in nothing but gym shoes and shorts
and ran round the head of Poole harbour and over the
hills to Swanage. Then along the top of the cliffs to
Old Harry and back along the coast to Studland. Then
up into the top of the Purbeck hills, and right along
the whole line of Purbeck to Corfe where I had a light
meal. And then along the crest of the hills again to
the top of Creech Barrow and then back here past
Wareham and Arne—right across country the whole
day. It was 32 miles in all, the longest cross-country
I have ever done, and so it is not surprising that my legs
feel a little stiff to-day. But it was glorious—lovely
views all over Dorset.

" You may be quite sure that before going on any
sort of job I shall let you know at home what I can
about it, and when it is. The moral support of your
thoughts and prayers is too big a thing for me to go
without, and so you may be sure that before going out

on any sort of job you will know something about it. There is, too, also the distinct possibility that we might move to other waters to operate—a long way away— and I would almost certainly see you before that. One day last week we sailed to Portland (spent the night in Weymouth Harbour) and had the boat tested on the D.G. range for magnetic mine effect. The result was absolutely nil—she has no influence on them whatever."

Whilst they were making preparations and undergoing training in Poole Harbour a gunnery representative came down and fitted the *Maid* with a strange weapon, which was duly fired for the first time. Graham was sitting on the side of the craft, contemplatively smoking his pipe and watching the proceedings. The blast bowled him over and when he recovered his senses he found himself minus both pipe and pants! The incident sounds as though this may have been their first acquaintance with the newly designed rocket projector.

The training was now complete and an opportunity for action occurred. By reason of strict censorship prevailing at that time Geoffrey was not able to refer in his letters to what took place on this operation, and so it is better that it should be described by Prout, assisted by Tom Winter, both of whom took part therein. Proutie writes :—

" The targets for the proposed raid were a large enemy liner carrying valuable cargo, and two smaller enemy craft that would be of great use to the Navy. These were anchored in a distant port and it was proposed to capture them in some way and bring them to British waters. The prospect thrilled the crew of the *Maid*, for it presented them with an opportunity to emulate their hero Drake in a cutting-out expedition. During preliminary planning, it was soon realised that the crew were far too few for the task. Military or naval assistance was impracticable. Gus therefore decided to invite selected Britishers to ' come to a party.' No one who received the message knew what the 'party' involved, but all knew it meant high adventure and everyone responded. It is to the great credit of those gallant fellows that they did not know what was in store for them until they were at sea, but were prepared to risk their lives for their country on an unknown project.

"Great credit must also be given to those nameless few who 'prepared the ground.' Without their efforts the operation could never have succeeded, and at considerable hazard they were responsible for enabling plans to be made that reduced risk to a minimum.

"A powerful tug was chartered, together with a smaller one, and both sailed, timed to arrive alongside the enemy at the darkest hour of the darkest night of the moon. Gus commanded the whole expedition, with Apple second in command. Graham commanded the smaller tug. The crew of the *Maid* were distributed as follows : with Gus were Apple, Andy, Denis Tottenham, Ernest Evison, the cook, André Desgrange, 'Haggis' (the nickname of Gus's batman) and myself ; and with Graham were Tom Winter and Buzz Perkins. The volunteers were divided between these parties. The tugs were manned by their own crews, who had volunteered with alacrity for the job.

"A heavy swell was encountered crossing the Bar, and the heavily laden tugs wallowed like pigs. This was most unfortunate for the volunteers, most of whom were not accustomed to small craft, and some of the poor fellows took fully two days to recover from their agony. As for the crew, if any of them had felt bad, they would not dare have shown it, for the wrath of Gus would have descended on them like an avalanche !

"Two days out disaster was narrowly averted. The diesel engine of the small tug developed piston trouble, and Graham signalled for assistance. She was then taken in tow whilst Tom Winter and the engineer worked on the engine. The small tug did not take kindly to being towed through the swell, and began to sheer alarmingly, in spite of the efforts of Graham and the very able Skipper to get her to answer her helm. Gus prompty rang to ' slow,' but Graham's vessel had developed such a sheer that her keel was showing out of the water, and her crew threw most of her provisions overboard before clambering on to her side in an effort to right her.   At this stage Andy, with great presence of mind, rushed aft on the large tug and cut the hawser with an axe.   Undoubtedly Andy's prompt action saved Graham's tug from total loss.

" Graham and Tom swam about retrieving their precious provisions and cases of beer, heedless of sharks or barracuda.   Eventually, reprovisioned from the large tug, and with her engine again in action, Graham's vessel got under way, and the voyage was resumed.

"A report stated that the enemy liner was secured by two heavy cables attached to her bow anchors, and by four lighter cables attached to her stern, whilst the smaller enemy vessels were anchored in the normal way, bow and stern.

" The plan had the simplicity of brilliance.

" 1. Both tugs were to act independently but simultaneously.

" 2. At a given signal they were both to enter the harbour and go alongside their targets, board them and make fast the towing cables, whilst selected parties (a) overcame resistance, and (b) placed cutting charges on the anchor and stern cables.

" 3. Once the cables had been made fast the tugs were to steam slowly ahead to enable the strain on the cables to cause the barnacled ships to ' spring ' from their moorings after the cables had been cut.

" 4. Completion of these tasks was to be reported to Gus on the bridge, and a single blast on his whistle was to be the signal for the blowing of the cables, and for the tugs to steam ' Full Ahead ' and tow their prizes out of the harbour.

" This plan was carried through with one small adjustment.   The Chief Engineer on the large tug had very wisely raised the question of the reaction of the native stokers to the 'big bangs,' and it was decided that I should go down the stokehole and control the stokers, for the vital importance of maintaining steam was indisputable. This meant of course, unfortunately, missing most of the fun, but I did not regret it, for those stokers worked magnificently.

" Every single man was briefed as to his exact duty, and rehearsal after rehearsal of the coming action took place on the outward voyage on both tugs. We arrived at our destination in pitch darkness shortly before midnight.

"Arms were issued, and last minute preparations made. The signal to go in was given, and the two tugs slid silently between the buoys towards the sleeping town and our prey. Once inside the harbour, the two tugmasters, by beautiful judgment, with engines stopped but still under way, brought their craft exactly alongside the target ships before they were heard and challenged by the look-outs.

"As the tug slid to within two feet of the liner's fo'castle Gus gave the order to board, and he led his party over the rails of the tug and the enemy ship and overpowered the look-out before the alarm could be given. The boarders were armed with ' coshes '—12 in. bolts covered with rubber and strictest orders were given to avoid the use of firearms.

" Once aboard, the raiders, about twenty in all, split into small parties to carry out the tasks allotted to them. Gus, followed closely by his diminutive bodyguard ' Haggis,' led his party quickly through the ship and captured the bewildered crew without a shot being fired. Only one blow was struck, and that was when one of the volunteers found an enemy officer ' looking aggressive.' The poor wretch did not look very aggressive after a tap with his assailant's ' persuader.' From the bridge Gus was able to see Apple and André fix their charges to the heavy anchor chains forward, and Andy and his party heave aboard the heavy hawser and make it fast to the bollards. The prisoners were driven into the after dining saloon, and astern John Eyres and

Desmond Long placed their charges on the mooring cables. On the tug the Master had eased forward with the engines just turning over, and was looking expectantly towards Gus on the bridge. Below in the tug, the Chief and Second Engineers were waiting for the clang of the telegraph and every ounce of steam and every revolution they could coax out of the 2,000 h.p. engines. In the stokehold I was telling the sweating stokers the tale as I had never told it before, and promised them a big ' dash ' if they worked well. My powers of persuasion were considerably assisted by a tommy gun and a Colt .45.

" Gus's shrill whistle pierced the silence and immediately the ships and harbour were shaken by a series of tremendous explosions. The telegraph clanged in the engine room of the tug, and the Chief opened the throttle wide. The powerful engines shook the tug as she strained and pulled at her huge burden, and the water was churned up into a phosphorescent race by the thrash of her propellers. The liner did not move. In the silence that followed the explosions Apple's clear voice was heard ' I am laying another charge.' One of the forward charges had failed to ignite and Apple, realising that the whole success of the operation depended upon him, rushed forward and laid another charge with a short fuse on the huge anchor chain. After what seemed an eternity Apple's voice rang out again ' I am going to blow.' Unable to get back to proper shelter he crouched behind a nearby winch. A blinding flash and a huge explosion followed immediately, the tug's propellers thrashed again, and the huge liner lurched and began to slide forward. A mighty shout rang out from the bridge : " My God, she's free.'

" Responsibility now shifted to the Tug Master and the Chief Engineer, and they acquitted themselves splendidly. By superb seamanship the Master towed his unwieldly prize through the narrow channel to the buoys, against a severe cross current, whilst below the Chief and Second broke all the safety rules of the

Mercantile Marine as the engines threatened to shake themselves out of their beds. The black stokers worked like demons and I almost felt like kissing them—but not quite !

"Pandemonium reigned ashore. Immediately after the detonations were heard the anti-aircraft guns went into action and blazed into the sky, the explosions having been mistaken for bombs from raiding aircraft. It was not until daylight came that it was realised on the shore that the steamers had gone in the night. It was as well that the 6 in. guns covering the harbour had not opened fire because the most powerful gun aboard the tug was a Bren !

" In the meantime, the smaller tug, whose Master had matched the skill of his colleague on the larger vessel, had come alongside her target, preceded by Graham and Tom Winter who had launched collapsible canoes from their parent ship, and had boarded the enemy vessel from them. On board they had found the watchman, who had challenged them, and who, confronted by two men with knives in their teeth and truncheons in their hands, took one horrified look and promptly dived overboard and swam for the shore.

" Finding no further opposition, Graham and Tom at once laid their cutting charges on the anchor chain and stern cables. At this moment the remaining two members of the boarding party came aboard from the tug and made fast the towing cable. The tug then went slowly ahead and took the strain on the cable. After making sure that the ship was actually in tow Graham and Tom fired the charges, the tug went ' Full ahead ' in exactly the same way as the larger one was doing in the case of the liner.

" Just as they got under way they heard the tremendous explosion from the liner and were overjoyed to find that all was well with Gus and his party. A few moments later they saw the huge bulk of the liner silhouetted in the dim light. She was moving faster than the smaller tug and reached the safety of the open sea ahead of Graham.

" Progress was slow against a strong flood tide, and when only two miles from the shore the engine failed once more. Whilst Tom and the engineer were trying to get some life out of the engine the tide was taking them back to the port which they hoped they had just left for ever. They found that the trouble was serious, and had to disconnect the connecting rod from one cylinder in order to get the engine to run on the remaining two. After three hours' work the engine started on the two cylinders and enabled the party to go ahead at one to two knots. Graham was determined not to lose the small craft which was lashed alongside the enemy vessel, and to help the disabled engine she was dropped astern of the main prize and towed in line ahead. Graham steamed straight out to sea for the remaining hours of darkness for a pre-arranged rendezvous with Gus some 200 miles distant. When daylight came they found that, in addition to their new prize, they were towing a sailing dinghy and a canoe! These they regretfully abandoned later as they could not spare the time to stop and get them inboard with a heavy swell running. The following day the second prize broke away and considerable time was lost circling to pick her up again. This accomplished, to the accompaniment of several very expressive remarks by all the party, it was decided to abandon the rendezvous and steam independently for the home port. Danger from British warships or submarines caused great concern, as the enemy vessel had her national colours painted on the funnel. Running short of water, they had the good fortune to sight a British cargo ship, which sheered off violently on seeing the enemy colours! Fortunately, however, the Tug Master knew the British ship and her Master which by now was approaching warily with her guns manned. By means of morse he managed to make himself known and all was well!

" The Master of the British ship very sportingly offered to tow Graham's entire fleet, and in this way, in long line ahead, they all reached the home port before Gus, much to the latter's surprise and relief.

" Meanwhile, Gus's party, during the long slow voyage back to port cleaned up the liner and made all ship-shape. The enemy crew was put to work, a check made of her cargo, and on the bridge I laboriously typed out Gus's official report. Gus forbade any form of looting, the only exception being clean linen. ' Haggis ' had been appearing in clean shirts daily and Gus ordered him to unearth his hoard, which he confiscated and shared between Apple and myself, to the deep chagrin of ' Haggis,' who as a mark of protest appeared in a pair of very feminine unmentionables which he had ferreted out from somewhere !

" When both Gus and Graham's parties arrived in home waters they were very quickly intercepted and taken over by the vigilant Navy who never got over their astonishment at finding enemy ships manned by their own countrymen."

The raid took place at a time when the shortage of Allied shipping was acute. This very fine ship and the smaller craft were welcome additions to the hard-pressed Merchant Navy, whilst their valuable cargoes made an equally useful addition to the Home country's depleted stores.

CHAPTER IV

WEST AFRICAN ADVENTURES

In August 1941 reports were received that German submarines were using the river deltas in Vichy West Africa as refuelling depots for their Atlantic operations. It was decided to send out *Maid Honor* and her crew to reconnoitre this coast—a task for which the ship was admirably suited because of her non-naval appearance, and for which the training of the crew had perfectly fitted them. The whole crew of the *Maid* had looked forward to the adventure of taking this fishing boat under sail the whole way to West Africa, without making any use of the auxiliary engine, so avoiding attracting enemy submarine activity. To Geoff's intense disappointment it was ruled from Headquarters that owing to the great importance of the mission to be carried out, the first and second in command should travel separately. Owing to the difficulty of carrying a large quantity of fresh water, the crew of the *Maid* was limited to five : Gus, Graham, Andy Lassen, Buz Perkins and Denis Tottenham. Geoffrey was to go out in advance in a transport and Prout was to take the rest of the party in another ship. All were to rendezvous at a camp to be constructed on a beach near Freetown by the first party to arrive.

On 13/8/41 Geoff wrote : " Everything is working up well, and, barring accidents, the show is definitely on. The Admiralty have given their approval, blessing and full co-operation. The kit, equipment and stores side of things has kept me tremendously busy for ten days, but is now well in control. I think the next time I see you I shall be able to say ' yes ' to all your questions as to ' have you got —— on board ' ! You may judge the pressure of the work by the fact that Gus had to go to Poole yesterday and was flown there and back by the

R.A.F.! By way of contrast, I am going down to Poole late to-morrow night on a lorry with about three tons of food stores, etc."

Prout describes the departure of the *Maid* as follows : "At last all was ready for the ship to sail, and she dropped her hook off Stakes Buoy while the crew went ashore for a farewell lunch at the Antelope. 'Pop' gave us a magnificent meal, honoured by the presence of the Brigadier (C. McV. Gubbins, c.m.g., d.s.o.), 'Franco' insisted on piloting the 'yacht' out free of charge, and in due course the whole party went out to the *Maid* and sailed out to Old Harry Rock, toasting success with Pop's very excellent champagne. A lady standing on the shore at Sandbanks waved again and again. She was Gus's Aunt, there to wish Godspeed to all aboard. The moment for parting had come, and the shore party transferred to the Pilot Boat. With many waves and exhortations the *Maid* gradually disappeared behind Old Harry, watched by a silent Blake, who never took his eyes off his beloved ship until she was out of sight.

" On the way back Franco relieved the inevitable reaction by getting mixed up with the Brigadier's rank, and bluntly informed him that he could not make out all those red.tabs, and that if he called him 'Cap'n' that would be good enough ! The Brigadier readily agreed to his change of rank, and so we returned to harbour.

" In the evening Apple and I took our minds off the ship by indulging in a colossal rag with Pop's daughter and niece. Pop named it the Battle of Poole, and Blake looked on and said, ' They there maidens—'tis astonishing what they can do to-day ! '

" Before I left England I found myself hauled over the coals by the Brigadier for stealing a suit of sails from a sister ship of *Maid Honor*. This crime had

----

been committed at dead of night under Gus's most forcible orders, under pain of hanging from the sprit. Gus, of course, was on the High Seas when I stopped the inevitable rocket. Gus had assumed the autocratic powers of the Sea Captains of old. None of the crew possessed any rights at all, although he later made a concession to Apple, who was granted the right to eat ! "

On 15/8/41 Geoffrey wrote a few minutes before he embarked : " Just a wee note to let you know all's well. I shall be going along to report to the Embarkation Officer in about half an hour. Thank you all so much for the send-off you gave me, and for the family prayers at home—they are, and will be, a great source of inspiration and strength. I do pray that you all keep well and out of harm's way and am already looking forward to seeing you again in the spring or early summer. Goodbye for the present and God bless."

Geoff's transport turned out to be the P. & O. liner *Strathmore*. The last time he had been aboard her was in August 1937 when she appeared cruising off Dubrovnik in the Adriatic where we were staying, and he swam out and boarded her. She was like an old friend, being almost identical with the *Strathallan* on which we sailed in 1938. Consequently Geoff had quite a *de luxe* voyage to West Africa. Only one incident provided any excitement. " We had a promise of some fun the day before yesterday, but nothing came of it. One of our escorting ships suddenly shot off to the flank and dropped a ' stick ' of depth charges, circled round, and then dropped a few more. We never knew what it was he heard, or thought he heard, but I don't think anything came of it. I am afraid that in any case my sympathies would be mainly with the wretched chaps under the surface, having a pretty good idea what it would be like ! "

PLATE X

Geoffrey—British Expeditionary Force, 1939

By courtesy of Bacon & Ismay Taylor

F

Here are his first impressions of Freetown in August.
" Well, I am here at last! I came ashore from the
ship about 10.00 a.m. to-day—although we arrived
here at 4 yesterday we could not land until to-day.
Freetown gives me mixed impressions. It is very one-
eyed, ramshackle, and quite an outpost of the Empire.
Apparently at this time of the year it rains almost continually (three-quarters of every day) and this is the
worst month. It has teemed down all day to-day in
bucketsfull and apparently three days ago they had
9 inches of rain in the day!! Yesterday they had 4
inches. Naturally everything is very damp and humid,
and when it isn't raining, a dense cloud of steam arises
from the earth, roofs and roads, etc.

" I have made very good arrangements for the
accommodation of the party. We shall be right out at
the end of Cape Sierra Leone, about nine miles out of
Freetown, and actually on the edge of the beach and
about three miles from the golf club. It will be cool,
as there is invariably a sea breeze, healthy, and will
offer good opportunities for exercise on the beach, in
the sea, etc. We are having special huts put up for us
by the Navy on our own chosen site, and will also
have a few tents, and will mess in the naval messes
which are very close. I think it will prove almost an
ideal arrangement for the dry season.

" September 29th—Lagos. Here I am seeing a bit
more of the West Coast! I think it has been rather a
mistake to come here as I am afraid it has rather
changed my opinions about Freetown, with which previously I was prepared to be satisfied. There is as
much difference between Freetown and Lagos as there
is between Wigan and Harrogate! I wish I were staying
here but am returning—probably by air—in two or
three days. There are wonderful facilities here for
Europeans, including riding, polo, racing, tennis, squash,
sailing, etc. Lovely houses and gardens, and I am staying in one of the most lovely ones, with one of the most
important people in Lagos! This is a most comfortable

house and I have had my first hot bath since leaving England. However, the mosquitoes here are much more active and very numerous—as, I believe, are various other pests. Lagos is in the midst of swamps (it is actually on an island) and is entirely surrounded by lagoons. Rainfall is less here (only 80 inches) and the weather is pleasant (comparatively) at present. However, normally the climate here is worse for Europeans than Freetown, the average humidity being 98.

" When I arrived at Lagos, I got the best piece of news I have ever had in my life, that is, that Graham and M-P. and the others have arrived at Freetown after an ' excellent ' voyage. Not having seen any of them yet (they arrived two days after I left Freetown) I don't know any more about their voyage than that. But I was enormously thrilled and literally shouted with joy ! I have thought about them continually in the last four weeks, and even dreamt of them at least every other night. You will agree with me that it is a very stout effort indeed. I don't think it would be exaggerating to say that it is one of the finest efforts of its kind in recent years."

A very remarkable achievement it was indeed for so tiny a sailing boat. Gus had a great admiration for the Elizabethans—Drake was his hero—and this voyage and its mission was inspired largely by the exploits of Sir Francis.

The reunion when Geoff returned to Freetown was joyous. " It was grand to arrive here and find Graham and Gus and the others. They had a magnificent trip with no particular excitements and a great deal of interest. Gus had found Graham a magnificent first mate and was full of praise for his tireless energy and his seaman-ship. They were very warm at times, their record temperature being when the thermometer in the galley went off the top of the scale at 135° F. ! ! However, in spite of such things they were pretty comfortable, fed well, and had plenty of drinking water, and a lot of flying fish which landed on board each night.

"We are now living here in very pleasant surroundings, in tents right on the edge of the sea in a
beautiful tropical bay, with a clump of palm and banana
and coconut trees 50 yards away. A lovely site—we all
spend three or four hours a day in the sea swimming,
diving and swimming under water wearing goggles and
armed with fish-spears, etc. I think this is the most
lovely spot anywhere near Freetown. It really is
pleasant. At night we sleep in the tents under mosquito
nets, or else on the ship which has its mooring only a
quarter of a mile out in the bay. We eat in the local
officers' mess (R.A.)—they are a most awfully nice and
hospitable crowd and have been out here about ten
months. Most of them are Yorkshiremen (they were a
Leeds T.A. Battery!) and one of them is John Davy
who is about twenty-six and newly married and lives
in Linton on the Common in the house next to the
Hudsons ! ! ! Isn't it amazing, for there are only eight
altogether in the mess. He is an awfully nice fellow
and I have seen a lot of him. Another in the mess is
Warren who lives at Knaresborough. He gets the
Yorkshire Post regularly and so I get frequent local home
news. Small world! Sleeping on board is really most
pleasant, as there are no mosquitoes, and thus no need
to use a net and so one is much cooler. Actually the
heat here isn't too terrible, and there is always the sea
(which, however, is lukewarm) when you can't bear the
heat any longer. We are about nine miles out of
Freetown and have our own car, but very little reason
to go in there. Thank heavens! Really this camp is
for us a sort of holiday and rest camp and we are just
ending one of our rest periods as we go out this afternoon for about a fortnight.

"We have been getting a tremendous amount of
exercise whilst on shore and I am now really fit and
getting a lot of the fat off which accumulated in the
first month out here. I get a half-mile swim and a
half-mile run every day before breakfast. Also I am
again very brown and thoroughly acclimatised to the
sun and immune to sunburn. We wear nothing all

day (aboard or ashore) but bathing trunks and sand shoes. Even topees are now dispensed with for normal working in the sun and they are only found necessary if actually sitting still out in the sun around midday. We have a pet monkey in our camp here, but don't as yet take him to sea ; an amusing little thing about the size of a small kitten. We call him Chico.

" Tornadoes are still common here, with a wind up to 60 m.p.h. and very heavy rain, lasting about half an hour. However, they should finish about the end of this month. We get them every two or three days, otherwise continual sunshine. There are lovely fireflies at nights all round the camp. Queer things, and the way their lights come and go makes one think one is seeing things. The sea provides perpetual new items of interest and contains the most weird and wonderful fish, with the most fantastic shapes and brilliant fluorescent colours, especially parrot fish, about two feet long with red, green and blue portions of the most brilliant shades."

Prout recalls : "At Lumley Beach in the friendly Gunners' Mess we made our first acquaintance with 2nd Lt. Warren, now Major Ian Warren, and later to become another member of Small Scale Raiding Force. Ian immediately fell for the *Maid* and lost no opportunity of entreating Gus to let him join. These entreaties gave birth to his nickname—' The Man.' Gus remarked to Ian's Commanding Officer that that b—— little man had been pestering him again, and from then on he was known to all as ' that b—— little man,' which in the course of time became just ' The Man.' ' The Man ' had a passion for a piece of music called *Stardust* and his presence in the Mess was always indicated by the gramophone wheezing out the masterpiece. Gus relieved the state of purgatory by breaking the record into little pieces over the culprit's head.

"At this time a ferocious looking Andy was seen searching for a pie-dog called ' Loopy,' and as Andy was carrying a nasty looking knife and a Colt .45 the future did not appear so good for Loopy. Buzz Perkins had told Andy that the dog had ' chopped ' his little monkey Chico, and from the shade of his tent was enjoying the spectacle of the future V.C. on the war-path.

" Life was further enlivened by my boy Tamara, who announced the fact that he could not work as he had been unfaithful to his wife, who had put ' ju-ju ' on him. I sought advice, and as a result administered the following ' anti-ju-ju ' mixture : Epsom Salts, syrup of figs, Eno's, and brimstone and treacle. The boy retired to the bush in a hurry, and some hours later returned to say that ' ju-ju am done finished.' "

On October 11 Geoff was thinking of the superiority of the much maligned English climate and wrote : " I suppose autumn is well on at home now and the trees and leaves must be in their finest colouring. It's a lovely season. What is it Keats says : ' Season of mists and mellow fruitfulness, close bosomed friend of the maturing sun.' The harvest too will all be in now I suppose and ploughing will be in progress. I wonder what sort of fruit season you had at home. And the evenings will be drawing in, with a feeling of frost in the air. And I suppose you will be getting the first of those strange evenings when the sun drops to the horizon with a bank of mist and is just a red disc, and there is a vague mistiness everywhere and a strange quietness. And celery for tea ! What a lot of character a country like this misses just because there are no seasons—no time of growth, no autumn and no dead winter when the trees are bare. Even the sun here is a different thing. At home the sun is always welcome and it's always pleasant to be out in it. Here there seems to be something so hard and pitiless and fiery about it (apart from its actual heat) and you always feel it's your enemy with no real friendliness and never the *warmth* that you get at home—just *fire*."

His letters at this time could tell but little of their adventures. Actually, at a later date we learned the party were searching the rivers, estuaries, deltas and lagoons for submarine bases, which were reputed to have been established by the Germans in anti-British Vichy territory on the West Coast, then violently hostile.

" I can tell you little about our activities. Life on the ship is incredibly full and we have no time off at all. It's funny, but it seems that the smaller the ship is the more there is to do on it, and the work when we are in port seems never ending, and when at sea is never ending ! I feel now very much at home on the ship as we have been out for two long spells lately, on one of which we covered over 1,000 miles. I can't tell you anything more about the trips than that, but they were of considerable interest and, according to official comment, of quite a fair amount of value, which is very gratifying as we are all putting a great deal of work into it. We are all working very long hours, but as there are no forms of relaxation here, other than swimming, that is no hardship, and our 'turning-round time' in harbour seems to get shorter and shorter ! I rather think we shall be having a move soon away from here, as our usefulness here must already be more or less over, and we shall move either to a home base or to some other place some distance away.

" The ship, you know, is by no means uncomfortable ; in fact, almost the reverse, and we are all of us happier at sea than ashore. Also she is not nearly as hot in this climate as you would expect, and it's always cooler at sea, so that the internal temperature is always between 80° and 90° F. We nearly always sleep on deck, but frequently have to beat a hasty retreat in the middle of the night as it still rains one night out of three, in spite of the fact that the rainy season officially ended at the end of September. I am, of course, now completely accustomed to the routine of ship's watches and no longer dislike even the 'graveyard' (12.00—3.00 a.m.) and 'dog' (3.00—6.00 a.m.) watches. Our watches at sea are three hours on and six off, but most of the six off are concerned with work about the ship. Sleep is the only thing one really misses, and we usually have to be satisfied with six hours in the twenty-four, which is really hardly enough, but it is unavoidable. But we are all feeling very fit and well. I have had no sickness of any sort yet, and really the climate doesn't bother me at all. And if one really looks after oneself I don't see why it should. We have had two cases of fever (malaria) in the party (of thirteen) so far—one of them being in hospital at the moment. The first dose seems to knock one out for about a fortnight. The hospital is very good and clean. Our feeding on board is really excellent—our cook comes to sea with us and does remarkably well, considering the conditions. Of course, all food is dried or tinned, but one can eat an astonishing variety of good food out of tins. We always take lots of lime juice and fresh oranges, so there is no fear of scurvy. One of the things I look forward to most in getting back again is bread, as one gets rather tired of the interminable ship's biscuit as a substitute for it.

"Ashore we still eat in the hospitable gunners' mess here. They are a grand crowd of chaps and we have some most interesting conversations and discussions. Also when Graham and I are both there, the Yorkshire element in the mess is four (three Linton and one Knaresborough) and so we can more than hold our own against any other county present and quite rule the roost! The Major is quite a young man (about twenty-eight) and an awfully good sort. Graham is in great form and invaluable. He has an enormous capacity for work and is about the finest chap you could possibly have with you. Gus, too, flourishes and is as full of drive as ever, which is one of the reasons for my saying we are not likely to be here much longer, as, with the prospect of things slackening Gus is already pushing for a move to 'fresh pastures.' I shall have some most interesting tales to tell you on our return of our adventure.

"Two interesting ornithological notes, Ian. About three weeks ago when about twenty miles off the land two English swallows came on board about dusk and perched on the topmast truck. It was lovely to hear them twittering away in such an English fashion and to see them flying about the sails and rigging. After dark I climbed up to them, and although they did not appear at all exhausted, they allowed me to pick them up one at a time, examine them, and put them down again on their lofty perch without ever stirring an inch. Neither was ringed, and both were ' birds of the year.' They left the ship with the first light in the morning. We were sailing south at the time.

" The other episode was when we were about thirty miles off the mouth of a large river and sighted a huge mass of floating reeds—a floating island thirty or forty yards square that had apparently broken adrift from some swampy marsh up the river. But the astonishing thing was that it was covered with nesting sea birds (some tern-like sort of bird), still sitting quite happily on their nests, while their mates fished round about! As we approached all rose in the air with a terrific clamour!

" By the way, this morning I saw what looked like a normal English grey wagtail. Perhaps this is within their wintering area? I can still take no real interest in these African birds—the storks, flamingoes, herons, eagles, buzzards, vultures, cranes, terns, frigate birds, etc., and they all seem travesties of some English bird and almost repellent! I must be a very insular person!

" It is strange to think of November at home now— fogs and mists, the leaves off the trees, and frosty mornings. Here the weather gets better each day, the sea bluer and the surf whiter. But I would very gladly change it for your grey skies, rain and mists! I am continually thinking of you all, and all of us are constantly talking of ' home ' ! "

Not until his return home did we hear the story of these submarine hunting expeditions. Once whilst engaged on this work, they entered a creek in a Native State. Geoffrey and Graham took the dinghy ostensibly to purchase fresh vegetables and fruit at a port at the river's mouth, but in reality thoroughly to look over the place. They were met by a gold laced official in a

rowing boat with eight oarsmen, who finally only permitted them to land because they said the fruit was
wanted for a sick man. Whilst Graham purchased the
fruit, Geoffrey was cross-questioned: " What was the
name of the ship ? " " B.M.60." " What was the
Master's name ? " " Johnson." " What was the sick
man's name ? " " Green." " What was Geoff's
name ? " " Jones." " What was Graham's name ? "
" Brown."

Geoffrey admitted that in the heat of the examination
only obvious names would come to him, but he took
the precaution of naming people he could visualise and
to whom he could attach characteristics to help his
memory. He was then told that before the Government
would let the *Maid Honor* proceed it would be necessary
for them to be satisfied that fruit for the sick man
was the only reason for visiting the port, and that an
official would return with them in the dinghy to see
him.

Accordingly a gold-braided colonel went back with
them. Geoffrey at the stern managed to bungle the
approach to the *Maid Honor* in order to give Graham
time to leap out and get aboard before the colonel, and
warn Gus that his name was Johnson, that the sick man
was Green and that one of the crew must at once be
got into bed and his face whitened with flour ! All
this was accomplished by the time Geoff had brought
the dinghy round for a ' second attempt.' The colonel
was received in state with a double naval rum—and more
than one !—by which time friendly diplomatic relations
were established on a merry basis. He inspected the
sick man and agreed the necessity for the fresh fruit.
He wanted to examine the deck house but was told it
was sealed because it contained the mails for South
Africa, and could not on any account be opened. He
agreed. Actually the deck house was false and concealed their only gun—a Vickers Mark 8 2-pounder.
The deck house could only be entered from below and
was instantly collapsible by pulling a lever. The gun
was then ready for action at all angles.

In the stern four depth charges were concealed beneath fishing nets. Gus, questioned by Geoff when ordering them, had replied, ' If we can't knock a sub. out any other way, we shall heave these into the ocean. The sub. will then proceed to perdition, closely followed by ourselves.'

Early in November 1941, they decided to explore the delta and mouths of the Pongo River where it was credibly reported a German submarine base had been established. The *Maid* was left under command of Graham Hayes, whilst Gus and Geoff dropped off in a two-seater Folbot rubber canoe ten miles off the river mouth. The *Maid's* instructions were to return to the precise spot three days later, meanwhile cruising well out to sea. The two paddled towards the coast but found terrific surf, unsurmountable by their small craft, breaking on the ' bar.' It appeared an impossible task to cross this obstacle, but they decided to risk it and by incredibly good fortune found the only possible place to get through without catastrophe. They hid by day amidst the mango swamps, and amused themselves by playing chess with the mud banks marked out as a chessboard and with bits of twig fancifully shaped to represent the various chess pieces. They played in daylight waking hours until the maddening multitude of mosquitoes drove them well nigh crazy, or they failed to agree, under the ' biting ' provocation, whether a twig represented a Bishop or a Pawn ! By night they paddled up the various river mouths until they had satisfied themselves no German depot existed in that river delta.

One pitch black night as they were paddling up the delta, hearing strange jungle noises in the darkness, progress seemed to lag. Gus called to Geoff, who was at the bow, " Come, Apple, do your bit ! " Geoff replied that he was doing his bit and paddling hard but still they made no headway. Geoff peered forward to investigate and found a huge crocodile spreading itself over the bow and with rows of shining teeth within a couple of feet of where he was sitting. He gave it a terrific swish with his paddle and fortunately the brute dropped off without upsetting the canoe.

On the appointed day they paddled out and again safely crossed the bar. They had the mortification of seeing the *Maid* sail by without observing them, and again later in the day the same experience. Just before dark the *Maid* again appeared and, ' Oh, joy,' their signals were seen and heard. It was difficult to know whether they or Graham were the more relieved. Graham had had all his small crew on the look-out all day, and not finding the canoe at the appointed spot had searched for miles beating up and down the coast. The trouble proved to be that the small canoe lay so low in the swell of the water, her freeboard being only nine inches, that she was invisible from the *Maid* even at the short distance which separated their relative judgments of what was ten miles from the shore. When they climbed on board Graham held out his hand and remarked " Dr. Livingstone, I presume ! "

One night the ' Bullum ' came up and blew so hard that the gooseneck on the boom came away from the mainmast. All hands were on deck all night to rectify the trouble, while the storm blew itself out. Ernest's repeated cups of cocoa kept the crew going during a very trying time. Next day both German and British aircraft circled the ship without event, and later the *Maid* was stopped by H.M.S. *Dunedin*. The crew looked rather fearfully into the gaping muzzles of *Dunedin's* guns, but fortunately they had the correct signal, and were then treated with typical naval generosity in the way of supplies and cigarettes.

From time to time the *Maid Honor*, having a hull made of wood, needed careening and scraping to get rid of the sea worms which, if left alone, bored holes right through the hull. On one such occasion it was necessary to rivet a copper plate over a damaged portion. Before the job was finished the tide came in and flooded the hull. Graham was working on the job, finally under the water, and in order that he could remain immersed long enough at a time the others held his head down until he signalled he was at the last gasp. Graham at this time had a devoted and faithful little black boy as servant, who rejoiced in the name of " Liverpool Blackout." Wherever Graham went, " Liverpool Blackout " was sure to go. He watched this copper plating proceeding and Graham held under water, with the greatest distress until he could control himself no longer and pleaded " Please don't drown the ' Major '— please don't drown him ! " As a matter of fact, Graham at that time was a lieutenant but to " Liverpool Blackout " his hero was the principal officer of whom he had ever heard in the whole British Army.

A month before Christmas Geoffrey wrote : " Now it doesn't look as though we shall be pointing our ' sprit ' homewards quite as soon as I thought we should be doing as bright new prospects are opening up. However, don't worry, we shall be home in the spring as was originally promised. Actually they can't keep the ship out in these waters longer than that because of the danger of the worm—six months in these waters is about all a non-copper-sheathed wooden ship could stand.

"At the moment the ship is in magnificent trim. We have done an immense amount of work on her in the last two weeks, including careening (for the fourth time since she came out) and she is all stocked up for a three months' open sea voyage if necessary. Actually we are expecting to receive orders to move to Lagos any minute—if we do so I shall wire you about it. I expect we shall be then in that part of the world over Christmas. Strange to think of Christmas only being a month away as the weather is steadily getting better here. To-night is a lovely night. I have been lying on my back on the deck looking up at the mast and rigging silhouetted against the tropical stars and moon and listening to the gramophone. We have a very fine set of records of good music on board and they really are a delight. We have no dance music at all, but I find now that I prefer what we have got ! We always sleep on deck, although we frequently have to turn in for a shower of rain in the middle of the night. Actually out here at our moorings the nights are very pleasant and quite cool (one is quite glad of a single blanket before dawn) and there are no flies nor mosquitoes.

" Graham and I always sleep alongside each other by the wheel aft. We have both had a spot of ear trouble lately and have been off swimming for about a week— nearly better now though. It was caused by water in the ears due to diving under the ship to cut loose a rope that got badly tangled in the propeller. It was quite a tricky and rather a frightening job as it was at night and the propeller is about 8 ft. down and right back in under the stern of the ship. It took us about two hours continuous diving and cutting with a razor-sharp blade before we got it all clear and freed the propeller. I think the continual immersion and the pressure forced the water into our ears. In future I shall wear plugs.

" Life out here is proving very cheap. I have not drawn any of my pay at all since leaving England and am still living on the £45 that I brought away with me. Actually, if you don't smoke or drink there is literally nothing to spend money on here—except for sweets ! Also you wear practically no clothes at all so never need to buy any. When on board literally the only clothes I wear from dawn till dusk are a pair of underpants and a pair of gym shoes. Nothing else at all, and so of course we are all as brown as berries now. At night when at sea on watch I wear a pair of long grey trousers and my ' Rastus ' sweater and am then plenty warm enough, even at the look-out post at the mast-head.

" We are now to all intents and purposes Navy ! All our contacts out here are with the Navy (with the exception of when we eat ashore in the Gunners' Mess). We come directly under the C. in C. for orders, and in all respects are treated as Navy. We also draw naval food supplies, and very good they are too. We always have a 10-gallon barrel of lime juice aboard (naval). Apart from that the only other beverage we have on board is naval issue rum of which we always have a gallon jar. I suppose it is the finest stuff of its kind in the world and we always keep it for emergency use, or rather ' hardship ' use, and when wet through or chilled and very tired it is a remarkably warming drink.

" We all took a day off last Sunday, the first for two months. It felt very strange and we all felt very ' flat ' doing it—it felt such a complete waste of time, and actually we were very glad to get back to work again yesterday on the ship. We had a rifle shooting match (teams of six) against the local Army Ordnance people and beat them very easily. Graham was the crack shot and we beat them in every event, and took first three places in the aggregate.

" It is astonishing how much work there is to do on a ship of this size, and the work literally seems to be never-ending—although I must say that the ship is in such good trim at the moment that the work is (temporarily) as nearly finished as ever it will be. But there will always be painting, rope work on the rigging, sail stitching, stowing, cleaning, sorting out, navigating, and trying to learn more and more about seamanship ! This really is as full-time a job (in daylight hours) as you could conceive, which is a very excellent thing in this place, and which, coupled with the hard physical work we do, is what I think is keeping us all so fit.

" Well, it's five to nine and that's bedtime in this country when you get up at 6. I'm afraid my letters at present are very scratchy, but with not having had news of you for so long, and with the very strict ban on what we can say about our and other people's doings in this part of the world, there is really very little to say.

" I suppose this letter will reach you around Christmas and so it brings you my very best Christmas wishes. I shall of course, be continually thinking of you all, and more than ever over Christmas. I hope you all manage to be at Linton for it—at any rate, I shall imagine you all there and will be wishing you a very happy time. We shall manage to have a jolly time on board—rather a novel one in fact. We have already got our Christmas dinner, as I happened to see a fine tinned ham in Freetown the other day and so bought it for our Christmas feast. Well, happy Christmas to you all ! Dearest love to you, Geoffrey."

Life, as Geoffrey said, was indeed very cheap in West Africa, and this aspect of existence suddenly occurred to Gus, to whom money meant little at any time. He therefore enquired of Prout, who was acting Paymaster, concerning the state of his worldly wealth. On receiving the answer, he drew fifty pounds, and departed on a shopping expedition accompanied by Prout who had been invited to join him. Gus spent his fifty pounds on ivory, borrowed a tenner from Prout, spent that on more ivory, borrowed another fiver to buy things that he really needed, and returned to the ship a happy man !

Then followed a letter from Geoffrey illustrating what mail means to a man overseas.

" Within twenty-four hours of sending off my last letter saying that I had had no mail for six to seven weeks a huge budget arrived—only just in time to catch us before we left Freetown, I hope for good. I immediately wired you saying 'All letters received up to 22nd October.' What a grand packet of mail it was too. On collecting my letters I abandoned myself to an absolute orgy of delightful reading. You have no idea what an excitement it is after a long wait, to get

----

PLATE XI

" MAID HONOR "

An impression of the converted Brixham Trawler which played so large a part in the West African adventures

With thanks to the artist, Reay Marshall, Royal Signals

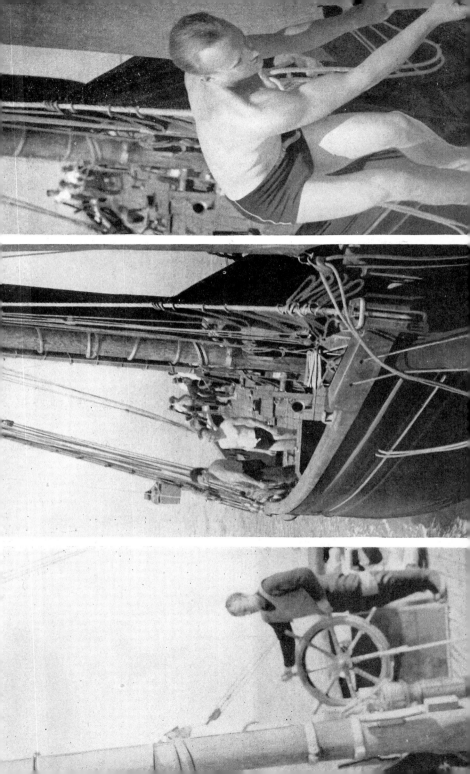

a budget of mail like that, especially as it is only the second mail received so far, and I immediately sat down on a grass verge by the side of the road in Freetown and began to read, but not until, with miraculous patience, I had cut open all the letters from home and arranged them in chronological order by means of the dates of writing. Thank you all very much for writing so much and for giving me so much news of everything you are all doing—it is all read and re-read and committed to memory with the greatest enthusiasm. The budget was of eighteen letters."

A description of life at sea on the *Maid* follows, together with this word-picture : " We have no ration on drinking water when at sea, which is a great boon, as each drinks between 1 and 1½ gallons a day out here all told. No other fresh water at all is allowed though, except half a cup of water a day for shaving. We all shave each day even when at sea. That half-cup goes a long way too—the technique is as follows. First you do your teeth in it (dipping the brush in, spitting over the side, and washing the brush in salt water before putting it back in the fresh water). Next you shave, then you have a complete bath in it, by dipping the soap in it, rubbing the soap over your body till it's dry, re-dipping the soap, etc., until you are completely soaped over, and then using the remaining few drops to get a lather up, finally swilling down with salt water. Believe it or not, it can be done and very well too. Try it sometime, but remember, only half a cup !

" For the last fourteen days we have been at sea, as we left Freetown on the 30th November. At present we are lying absolutely motionless and becalmed ten miles off Lagos. After a voyage of some 1,300 miles it

- - - - - - - - - - - - - - -

PLATE XII

LIFE ON BOARD THE " MAID HONOR "

*Photos by the late Capt. Graham Hayes, M.C.,
and found undeveloped in his camera
Reproduced by courtesy of his parents*

is a little trying to be within ten miles of our objective and to be temporarily unable to get there, as our motor has packed up, having run a bearing which can, however, be replaced in Lagos. Actually it packed up eight or nine days ago and so most of the voyage has been under sail only, but nevertheless we have got on quite well. However, it's an ill wind that blows nobody any good (I'm afraid ' wind ' is rather a poor word to use in the circumstances) as being becalmed gives us some spare time ! This is literally the first real opportunity I have had to sit down and write. Actually I am on watch at the moment (12.00 noon to 3.00 p.m.), but as the ship is so motionless that she won't answer her helm, and as it's no good keeping a look-out as even if one did see anything we can neither move away from it nor towards it, there is very little to do. So we sit and are slowly drifting away from our destination ! But it can't go on—I expect we shall get a sea breeze this evening that will take us in. This is the first time so far that we have been absolutely becalmed and motionless—sails flapping, spars creaking, and the ship rolling sullenly and stupidly in the swell.

" Most of the rest of the crew are dangling all sorts of inducements over the side on hooks to try and get the numerous small and large fish which are all around us to bite. As I write, sitting by the wheel and supporting this on the gunwale, I can glance over the side and see three or four small sharks and dozens of smaller fish. Just now a 6 ft. shark has swum idly under the ship—there is a great competition to get him—but I think he is going to be too wily. The water is incredibly clear—a few minutes ago the cook dropped half a dozen tins overboard (debris from to-day's lunch) and we watched them sink flashing through the water for over two minutes, until they were so small they could no longer be seen. It made one quite dizzy to look down watching them—like looking over the top of a high precipice !

" This looks like some wind coming—I can see dark ripples on the water two or three miles away to starboard.

" . . . It was wind, and now I'm off watch (five past three) and the ship is beating up close hauled against the breeze and it looks as though we shall just make Lagos before dark. I hope so, as otherwise we shall have to anchor off for the night, and as that will be in about twenty fathoms it will mean some very heavy work on the windlass to get it up again to-morrow. It will mean night watches too, whereas we were all looking forward to a night's sleep snugly moored up in the harbour. One always feels a little short of sleep—you can't get more than six hours at night whichever watch you have, and it's only rarely that one can sleep at other times in the day. Also this trip we have had several little misfortunes with the sails and spars, and each time it has been at night so that three or four nights we have only had three or four hours' sleep, and have had some very heavy hauling and heaving to do between 2 and 5 a.m. ! Still it's all in the game. Apart from such things the voyage has been practically uneventful except for one great excitement when we killed our first shark. It swam up near us one afternoon and André harpooned it (with a home-made harpoon) and as we hauled it alongside Graham shot it through the head with his automatic. We hauled it aboard on a tackle eventually and it measured over 9 ft. and weighed about 200 lbs. A filthy brute, and as ugly as sin, and stank like a sewer ! It was impossible to feel any pity for him, and after he was dead we hauled him up over the deck by his tail and Graham took some photos. We cut off the long fin of the tail and mounted it on the end of the bowsprit. It is supposed to bring good luck and good winds, and in any case it looks jolly fine. Graham says they had one on the *Pommern* and everyone was most proud of it. It was rather a joke catching the shark as about two minutes before I (at the wheel) had said to André, why not have a swim alongside the boat as we were only doing about 1½ knots ! But he didn't feel inclined. I should have gone in if it hadn't been for the fact that I was at the wheel ! Since then there has been remarkably little swimming from the ship when in deep waters—in fact none at all. I don't think the shark was big enough to have done any real damage, but he could certainly have given one a very nasty bite.

"A fish that almost constantly keeps us company at sea is the porpoise, and they are frequently sporting all round the bow within two or three feet of the ship—a lovely sight as they are extraordinarily beautiful swimmers and incredibly fast. By night they really are an astounding sight. As you know, the water here is extremely phosphorescent, and on a dark night you will suddenly see half a dozen or so apparent torpedoes streaking through the water from the beam straight towards the ship, leaving a 25-yards-long trail of brilliant light behind them. Then on reaching the ship they will swerve and dive, dash a zigzag all round the bow in a maze of dazzling phosphorescent light, so that you are astonished they don't either collide with each other or with the ship, and then tiring of the sport, they will dash off or else dive deep down, their light trails finally disappearing in the black water under the bow. That description does poor justice to a sight which is really extraordinary, and which never fails to interest and excite one, from the moment of the look-out's first yell of ' Porpoises ' until the last flash of phosphorescence dies away !

" I have been learning a great deal of navigation on this last voyage and can now take sun and moon sights with confidence and place the ship to within a mile, wherever she is. Star sights I am not really conversant with yet, not the least difficulty being spotting the stars ! I sometimes wish I had taken a bit more interest in Astronomy during my spare time at Bootham. I find navigation a fascinating subject and one that brushes up my Maths. (especially Trig.) considerably. It is amazing how little one has forgotten when one gets down to it. It was a source of no little satisfaction to Gus and me this morning (we have navigated between us) when we hit off Lagos to within five miles after an ocean voyage of fourteen days and 1,300 miles with no

sight of land at all since Cape Sierra Leone. But, as
you will imagine, there was some pretty careful checking
and re-checking of calculations and courses yesterday,
and an eager and expectant watch at the mast-head at
dawn this morning to see if it really was the land we
expected that came up, and not the Niger River or
Cape Town or anything else ! But all was well.

" The stars here are very unfamiliar—the Plough is
very low in the northern horizon and the only con-
stellation known of old is Orion which is usually
directly overhead and a magnificent sight. It must be
well south to you. I haven't yet spotted the Southern
Cross although it should be visible south of about
20° N.

" Don't worry about my health. We are all keeping
surprisingly fit, and really feel quite well, except for a
certain amount of physical lassitude and laziness. You
don't feel that you want to be energetic and run around
and throw your weight about in this country as you do
in northern climes. You find you don't do any more
physical work than you need, and what you do do tires
you rather. But we are all in good health—no fever,
dysentery, etc., and I am not really putting any fat on
now that I am on the ship. Hands are very hard and
horny with working the ship ! Of course this is the
healthiest way of living out here—to be on the sea so
much—it's so much cooler and fresher. Thanks for
the warning about jiggers—none of us has got them
(miraculously) and we all take good precautions. In
fact ashore I am quite fussy about wearing slippers and
not going about with bare feet !

" The Mess at Freetown (Gunners') was very sorry
to see us go and gave us a great send-off. They really
were extraordinarily kind to us during our stay there,
and did everything for us—in fact we were very much
in their debt—and yet on leaving they presented the
ship with a beautiful silver tankard ! And indeed the
presentation, if any, should have been the other way
round.

" What a week of news it has been—every evening
one of the crew listens in to the B.B.C. 9 p.m. news
bulletin and then writes out a ship's news bulletin
which all can read. I was amazed to hear of the
Japanese sudden entry into the war and since then we
have all waited for the news bulletins with terrific
interest. What little swines those Japs are. It is
astonishing that they should of their own accord make
an unprovoked attack on Great Britain and U.S.A.
together. At first, with the initial disasters I took rather
a gloomy view of the situation, but now, especially with
U.S.A. completely in, I think it will shorten the war.
The Japs seem to have made long preparations for the
attack. Terrible about the *Repulse* and the *Prince of
Wales*—it shows the vulnerability of battleships against
determined air attack. I expect too that the Swordfish
you are helping to produce and other naval aircraft
will be very busy out there. The *Prince of Wales* was
in Freetown when on her way out to Singapore about
six or seven weeks ago. I met several of her officers
and crew and had a very good look at her. It seems
awful to think of her now sunk.

" Things in Russia and Libya seem to be going
magnificently. Good to think of the Jerries on the run.

" We have changed our clocks a couple of hours in the
last two weeks and are now on British Summer Time as you
are. Distances are so vast here that time changes almost
' wisibly ' as one moves about. Dawn and dusk are appre-
ciably earlier or later each day as one goes east or west.

" We are now snugly anchored in Lagos river—it is
strange to feel the boat quite still again, sails all stowed
and deck awnings up, etc. After all we had to have a
tow in, as wind and tide were dead against us. We
got in about midnight. It's nice to think of a few nights
now with no night watches and sound sleep without
the ship bucking and pitching in the swell. Bed at 9
and up at 7 will be the order of the night for a bit. It's
lovely too to have fresh food. We have just had fresh
grapefruit, steak and tomatoes and fresh pineapple for
lunch. Small native canoes have been around us ever

since we came in, and we have baskets of pineapple,
oranges, bananas and grapefruit on board. As I write
there is a canoe alongside with all sorts of native work—
leather cushion covers, knives, bones, carvings, etc.,
and several of the crew are clustered round it bargaining.
There is a great deal of laughing and amusement.
These chaps can literally be bargained down to a quarter
their price. At the moment ' Buzz ' is bargaining for a
worked leather cushion cover for which the native is
asking £2. ' Buzz ' is offering six shillings, fourteen
cigarettes, and two pairs of old (unwashed) pyjamas !
And he'll get it ! As a side-line he is also offering to
jump in the canoe and sink it if he doesn't ! "

Geoff's letter from Lagos on Christmas Eve 1941
said : " Gus wrote the following poem whilst we were
fretting to be away from Freetown on our task. I
wonder how you like it. I think it rather good. It was
inspired by the fact that the *Maid* was moored to a buoy
right in the middle of the channel, where the ebb
stream flowing away out of the river mouth roared
past her at about 5–6 knots, leaving her tugging rest-
lessly at the buoy cable to get away ! "

EBB TIDE

The ebb tide dashing out to sea
    Sighs and surges under me,
Sets the captive vessel dancing
    Like a restless pony prancing,
        Fretting to be free ;
Sidling, edging, plunging, shearing,
    Like a maddened pony rearing,
        Frantic to be free.

Hear the tide call ' follow, follow,'
    West towards the sun,
Sure as hawk and swift as swallow,
    See the ebb tide run ;
Over shoal and shallow thrashing,
    Through the deeps and channels dashing,
        See the main ebb run !

All can hear but few may answer
  When the ebb tide calls,
Strong as lion, light as lancer,
  Still the ebb tide calls ;
Follow where the sun is sinking,
  Where the first pole star is winking
  As the darkness falls.

The ebb tide dashing to the sea
  Slackens, slackens under me,
And the restless vessel steadies
  In the currents' dying eddies,
  Draining to the sea.
Through the darkness falling, falling,
  Hear the echo faintly calling
  ' Follow and be Free ! '

G. MARCH-PHILLIPPS

" Rain here now is very scarce (for the past month or so) and, on board, when we do get a downpour it is enthusiastically welcomed. On the way here we had one such. It is a type of tornado and is locally called a ' Bullom.' The first you know is that you see a great mass of inky black clouds coming up over the horizon. These work up *against* the wind with tremendous speed. Just before they reach you the prevailing wind dies away completely and then the ' Bullom ' hits you. It starts with 5–10 minutes really hard wind of full gale force, then a torrential downpour of very cold rain. Meanwhile the wind screams and howls around the rigging, visibility is reduced to about 50 yards and the ship tears along through a boiling sea at 10 or 12 knots. It really is most exciting and one of the few interests of sailing in this part of the world. Just at the end of the rainy season ' Bulloms ' are very common (two a week or so), but now are very scarce. Still, they are certainly exciting, and when they come up at night and you don't get much warning you have to be pretty nippy, getting the light weather canvas in, the storm sails rigged. You have to be continually on the alert for them. Actually, they rather spoil the sailing as they are usually followed by a dead calm and it takes several hours before the wind re-establishes itself in the normal quarter. But the greatest thrill of the ' Bullom,' when we have been a number of days at sea without fresh washing water, is the rain, and when that breaks we all rush about the deck, stark naked, with cakes of soap, having a most glorious lather up and bath in the downpour, and simply shouting with glee ! "

In a letter of the same date to his sister he described his shipmates. " I don't think I have ever told you who our regular crew now consist of—nine of us in all, and as, when at sea, the people one is with are practically one's whole life, you might be interested to know about them. Also when I refer to anyone in future letters you will have some idea whom I am talking about.

" We are three officers on board—Gus (Captain), Graham and I—all of whom you know. Theoretically, I am first mate, and Graham second, but that is rather a misnomer, as he is much the better seaman and is considerably more use on the ship than I am, so that really the true position is that Graham is mate and I am second in command of the ship to Gus, or ' first officer.' Then there is Tom Winter, who was a sergeant in Graham's parachute battalion. He is a special protégé of Graham's and the two always work together. He is a very good scout, and has seen a lot of different parts of the world and done a lot of tough jobs, and is an expert engineer.

" Next comes André Desgrange, who is *my* special protégé, always works with me, and is one of the very finest chaps with whom I have ever had anything to do. He was with me on the *Tigris* for that party (I extolled his virtues after that, you remember), is a Frenchman, was a deep sea diver in the French Navy before the war and is also a good engineer, especially regarding steam and steam turbine engines. He is big, strong as a horse and has black curly hair and a perpetual grin !

He speaks no English at all (even after six months with us) but is the most un-French-like Frenchman in his characteristics that you can imagine, as, in an emergency he is absolutely cool, unexcitable and collected. He never gets flurried, and is always cheerful and willing for the hardest and filthiest jobs there are going. He really is a wizard and I feel tremendously fortunate to have such a stalwart with me as my right-hand man. He is well educated and was a C.P.O. in the French Navy. Age 30.

"Also we have Andy Lassen—a Dane—who is a crack shot with any kind of weapon, and a splendid seaman.

" Then there is Denis Tottenham, who is aged 24, and a good seaman. He has done a great deal of sailing, is 6ft. 4in. in height, and is in charge of the third watch. Graham and I take the second and first respectively, each watch being of two men. André, of course, being the second man in my watch.

" Then there is ' Buzz ' Perkins, the youngest of the party, who is a very sound lad, very keen and willing and tough. He is the nephew of a Major at H.Q., and it was he who put us on to him.

"And finally, there is Ernest Evison, the cook (whole-time job when we are at sea), who in his job is invaluable and unbeatable. He is most excellent. Scrupulously clean and punctual, he is an excellent cook, with a good secondary education, stands the sea perfectly, and was trained in France and Switzerland, and so speaks good French and German. He comes of a long line of cooks (father, grandfather, etc.) and, as it is his profession, he takes a real pride and interest in his job. He is only a young chap (23) and was secured for us by Prout, who has known him personally for some time. We are very lucky there.

"And so you see we are a very well-fitted crowd and really get on extremely well together, a very important thing in so small a ship and under such conditions."

On 30/12/41 Geoff wrote : " The Ski Year Book arrived on Christmas Eve (very appropriately!) and gave me much pleasurable reading, although I was very saddened by the ' Roll of Honour.' I suppose you have seen it too. Both Mike Anderson and David Wilson's deaths are reported, and there is an account of how the latter was killed. Jolly bad luck! What an astonishing number of the casualties were R.A.F., but I suppose flying and ski-ing tend to go together. Now four out of the five Cambridge team at Breuil in 1937 have been killed as, you remember, Wrenford was killed just before the war. Also I note that Willi Walch, the Austrian, has been killed in Russia. He trained the university team at Davos in 1938 and was a very nice little chap and a superb skier. Granz, the German ski champion, has been killed in Russia too. I see that my great friend ' Noldi ' Kaech, the Swiss who was in Norway with us in 1939, is second Swiss Military Attaché in Berlin. I hope we don't bomb him.

" We went up to Olokemeji—a tiny little place in the bush on Christmas Day and had three nights there. It was a delightful change and really felt like a Christmas holiday. The only European dwelling there is the house we stayed in—it used to be used as a holiday house by the Governor of Nigeria, but after that was lived in by the Forestry Commissioners up there. A very pleasant house, and the country up there is very interesting—especially as it was our first experience of the African interior, which is infinitely pleasanter than this coastal strip, much healthier, and is a country of which one could get quite fond. It is much drier (*i.e.*, less sweaty) and quite cool at nights, when the temperature often gets down to 70° F. and you actually need a blanket most nights before morning. The mornings are really pleasant so that you feel quite fit, and, although it gets really hot at midday and in the afternoon (when you have a siesta) it cools off again nicely in the evening. There are also two small hills, and although they are densely covered with bush (' jungle ' to you) we managed to force our way up one of them one morning. It was pleasant to walk on a slope again after this pancake flat country around here. We had some rifles with us and shot some small game, but saw nothing bigger than gazelles. We hoped for some leopards, but none could be found. We tried crocodile shooting one day but the crocs. were apparently away for Christmas and didn't appear. However, we shot quails and guinea-fowl with some success. They were excellent eating. We dynamited fish twice—great sport and yielded a big catch of about 40 lbs. each day. The two best fish were two Nile Perch of $5\frac{1}{2}$ and $6\frac{3}{4}$ lbs.—quite big fish—countless varieties of fish, some foully ugly and fierce, but nearly all eatable. We had luscious fruits there which we picked straight from the forest trees—oranges, grapefruit, coconuts and tangerine as big as grapefruit, no pips, and full of juice—one of the loveliest fruits you could wish for !

" There were nine of us up there for Christmas—all men, except for the wife of the present occupier of the house. We had a very jolly Christmas Day (we arrived for lunch Christmas Day) and a grand Christmas dinner at night with turkey and etceteras, plum-pudding (on fire !), mince pies, etc., and all the additions of crackers, a Christmas tree (with presents !), chocolates, nuts, etc. Great fun, and all very unexpected.

" The experiments and training for which we went up there proved a great success too, so it was a memorable three days."

Soon after Christmas Gus received orders to bring his party home to carry out a policy of raiding against the enemy's Channel Coast. The *Maid* herself, her hull now unseaworthy for the long voyage home after her sojourn in tropical waters, regretfully was left behind—a bitter estrangement for her crew. Geoff came home in the cruiser H.M.S. *Mauritius*.

In recognition of the achievements in *Maid Honor* and particularly that in which the enemy liner was captured (described in the previous chapter) the *London Gazette* of 28/7/42 had the announcement :—

> *The King has been graciously pleased to approve the following awards in recognition of gallant and distinguished services in the field :—*

The Distinguished Service Order.

Major Gustavus Henry March-Phillipps,M.B.E. (39184), Royal Regiment of Artillery.

Bar to the Military Cross.

Lieutenant (acting Captain) John Geoffrey Appleyard, M.C. (86639), Royal Army Service Corps.

The Military Cross.

Lieutenant (acting Captain) Graham Hayes (129354), The Border Regiment.

Soon after his return to England Geoff received a command to attend an Investiture at the Palace for the bestowal of his first M.C. As will have been gathered from these notes he was always a very informal soldier and loathed ceremony—indeed he never had any soldierly training in the usually accepted sense of the term, having been called up straight into his commission and despatched immediately to France with his men.

Not so, however, his younger brother, by that time a Leeds University Training Corps cadet and very much steeped in drill and discipline. The latter was very anxious his elder, carefree brother should not disgrace himself at the Palace. It was an amusing experience on a country walk near home one afternoon shortly before the great day to see the cadet call the captain to order, select a telegraph post to represent His Majesty, the King, and demonstrate how the form of the ceremony should be accomplished and then to hear the cadet—' the lowest form of military life ' as he called himself—

practise the captain before the telegraph post—
'Advance three steps '—' halt '—' bow '—' stand to
attention '—' bow '—' retreat one step '—' right turn '
—' quick march ' !

The drill was effective and a day or two later a very
proud mother and father saw their elder son decorated
by His Majesty.

CHAPTER V

RAIDING ACROSS THE CHANNEL

AFTER THEIR RETURN to England Gus and Geoff were instructed to return to the south coast and carry out a plan they had worked out whilst in Africa to expand their Special Services Command operating under the Chief of Combined Operations (Lord Louis Mountbatten) and train a further band of hand-picked Commandos, mostly officers, to form a nucleus for a Small Scale Raiding Force against the coast of France, operating with motor launches capable of 30 knots and landing by means of special boats built to their suggestions.

On the 21st of March, 1942, Geoff wrote : " Gus and I drove down to Dorset to spend a day house hunting. We stayed in Poole at the old Antelope Hotel which was our shore H.Q. last summer. They gave us a great welcome. During the Friday's house hunting we located an eminently suitable and magnificent house—about seven miles from Wareham and ten from Poole. It is a large and very beautiful Elizabethan house and in every way ideal for our purpose. However, the Ministry of Health are also trying to get the house, and we shall have to fight them for it. But I feel that we shall win ! The house is very much in the country, in an excellent training area, and with beautiful gardens. The head gardener is staying on, and, in our waiting times, of which, I suppose there are bound to be a great deal, we shall, when not training, give a hand in the grounds and gardens. The house, after the owners go, will be almost fully furnished. Initially there will be about thirty of us living there, nearly all officers. You may know the house ? It is quite a show place, and very like that Tudor house near Windsor that is now an hotel where Anne Boleyn is supposed to have lived once—' Great Fosters,' Egham, isn't it ? Dorset-shire was looking lovely—a really spring-like day. In the woods we found primroses and lovely scented purple violets, and the gardens were full of crocuses."

Their choice fell on this place because of the secrecy it gave for their future training, being ten miles inland, remote in the country and yet accessible to Portsmouth, Poole and Portland for their future amphibious raids.

Their aim in their exercises was to become masters in the new technique of Combined Operations in small raids on the enemy coast, and when themselves experts to train a constant sequence of new-comers in this work—mostly officers who volunteered for the training—to handle boats in all kinds of weather, to navigate, to swim in full equipment with weapons held above the water, above all to develop initiative, self-reliance and self-confidence. For example, the troop dismissed from parade one afternoon would be told to reassemble at a spot a hundred miles away the following morning. How they got there was the individual's affair—he had 6/8 a day for food and how he fed thereon was his own business. The men were trained to value comradeship and friendship, and their training and expeditions were carried out in pairs, whether as scouts or on long assault courses or in attack upon the enemy, and as far as possible were given choice of companion. Punish-ments were avoided. If a man did not make the grade he left the Troop and that was all—very few ever left.

Long jumping was carried out over the moat filled with barbed wire ; rivers with live mines were crossed on rope bridges made up on the spot by joining lengths of toggle rope carried by each man ; apparently in-accessible coast cliffs were climbed by the help of ropes ; launching, sailing and landing exercises in the Channel were carried out in all weathers, stormy pre-ferred, in every conceivable kind of craft likely to be useful in small raids upon the enemy defences. On cross channel trips the sea often broke over the low racing craft shooting along at 30 to 40 miles per hour, and the men were wet through from head to foot for hours on end. So cramped was the space and so violent the motion that navigation could only be done by lying down full length in a space two feet high over the chart and under the low covered deck, wedged with elbows against the side.

It is interesting in looking back to note how this rigorous Commando training later inspired the training of the whole British Army as a means of developing the fitness and toughness of the ordinary recruit, and particularly of officer cadets.

At this time (June 1942) Geoffrey wrote : " Yes, I quite agree, Mummy. I think the opening of a second front at present would be absolute madness and would, I am sure, be doomed to failure, with most depressing results. I cannot understand the present publicity that is being given to the second front idea. Surely, if we were thinking of it as an operation in the near future we would not tell the world about it, and if we are not really considering it, the bluff that we are at present carrying out about it will be more damaging to us in causing lack of confidence, than it will be to the Germans, in causing them to take precautions against eventualities. No, I don't see it.

" Personally, of course, I still feel strongly that at the present time our contribution to the European situation ought to be in the nature of a vast number of small raids all up and down the length of the European coastline. I don't mean one raid a month as at present, which from a strategic point of view can really have no value at all, as the enemy, knowing how few and far between they are, can afford to ignore them—but small raids every night (possibly several a night), involving only a few British troops, and all over the whole length of the occupied coastline. Then the enemy would be forced to strengthen his coastal defences and make substantial alterations in the disposition of his forces in Europe."

Further on, his letter had a comic touch. " The farm here is owned by a man named S....—a good sort, though we hadn't met him until recently (as he

H

owns several farms and is not always here). When we were hay-making, a rather better dressed man than the average farmer came along, and so Francis Howard, wishing to enquire about rabbit shooting on the farm, went up to him and said, 'Are you old S....'s agent ? ' ' No,' said the man, ' I'm old S.... !! ' Since then, old S.... has sent in two lovely lobsters and a salmon for the mess and so now he is ' good old S....' By the way, one of the happy memories of our walking tour on Exmoor is the sight of The Lord Howard of Penrith dipping into a mess tin *with his fingers* and pulling out greasy pieces of fried bully beef ! "

The following letter supplies some detail of the Exmoor walk : " We have had some interesting training schemes to fill the time up and all last week were out on Exmoor and the North Devon coast on a special living out scheme. We were entirely independent, and living solely on a very concentrated special ration, and sleeping out under hedges, etc., just where we got to. The aim was to see if we could still march 30 miles or so a day without packing up. Quite a holiday except for carrying a 45-lb. pack and the rations—it was hell to walk past a pub and see them drinking beer and cider and to have to go on to the local duck-pond instead, chlorinate the water and drink it ! It was a scorching week but really was great fun. My party and I walked 120 miles in four days—Exeter, Lynmouth, Lynton, Ilfracombe, Barnstaple, Exeter. Mostly over rough ground and tracks. The rations turned out very well, and though we felt eternally hungry, we had plenty of energy. Poor Graham has had a ' nasty mishap,' as, apparently owing to being insufficiently filled, his stomach appears to have caved in and he can no longer eat a decent-sized meal without having violent stomach ache ! ! Mercifully, mine has responded to food again quite normally, only rather more so ! "

A constant sequence of training and raiding went on day and night, by land and sea. They had two fast motor boats allotted to their command. There came a time when Gus and Geoff were out in the Channel attempting to reach the Brittany or Normandy coasts whenever the nights were dark, and three or four times a week. Often mists, gales, currents or engine break-downs turned them back when a successful landing seemed almost certain, but often they landed and carried out a surprise attack here and there until the enemy, pin-pricked in so many points by these and other raids, of necessity had to double his guards and sentries along the whole Atlantic coast and thus immobilise troops he could well have employed elsewhere.

One such raid is very fully described in the official book *Combined Operations*, chapter 3, under the title " The Steel Hand from the Sea."   Geoffrey wrote a confidential account of that night's work for the reason stated at the end of his letter. It can be quoted here now, having been officially described in other words.

" I thought you would be glad to know that we had another successful little party the night before last and that this time we brought back seven prisoners—all without a shot being fired on either side ! We had no casualties except for two very minor ones—my ankle and Kemp's slight cut on the thigh—accidentally done in the landing boat.

" You remember I said that some time ago we went somewhere and were beaten by fog at the last moment, and, although we knew we were within a few hundred yards of our objective we couldn't find it ? Well, since then we have tried repeatedly to pull off this little job but always we either had breakdowns or impossible weather, but last Wednesday night, which was the ninth or tenth night on which we have tried this particular job, we got it in the bag.

" The job was to land on the Casquets rock, capture the lighthouse and buildings, take all inhabitants prisoner and bring away certain code books, documents and other naval papers. The station was being used as a naval signal station, and was entirely manned by German naval personnel—there were reported to be about six there. The job attained its full objective, as, besides our seven prisoners, we got the required code books, etc. Two of the prisoners were leading tele-graphists, and one had an iron cross. We used a landing party of twelve men, two of whom had to remain with the boat, so we actually attacked with ten.

" I navigated again for the whole job. It was pretty nerve-racking as it's a notoriously evil place and you get a tremendous tide race round the rocks. However, all went well, and we found the place all right, and pushed in our landing craft. My job in the landing and embarkation was bow-man, i.e., I was the first to leap for the rock, taking a light line with me, and then had to hold the landing craft up to the rock on the bowline whilst Graham, in the stern, held the boat off the rock with a stern-line and kedge-anchor he had dropped on the approach, so as to prevent her being dashed on the rock by the swell. When she was so held it was comparatively simple for the remainder to disembark with the aid of the bowline. There was quite a hefty swell surging up the rocks, and it felt pretty weird in the dark, but we got the whole party ashore safely. The boat was then hauled off the rock on the stern-line by Graham (who remained in her) and I handed over the bowline to the other man who was staying with the boat, and then she rode quite happily until our return.

" We had to climb through and over barbed wire entanglements, but finally gained the courtyard un-challenged and then each rushed our previously decided objectives. Mine, assisted by Sgt. Winter, was the main light tower itself. The door was open, and after a lightning ascent of eighty feet of spiral staircase we found the light-room empty ! The light was not on. The whole garrison was taken completely by surprise. I have never seen men look so amazed and terrified at the same time ! I suppose they wouldn't be expecting visitors for another month or so, and suddenly to have a rather rough looking party arrive in the middle of the night must have made them wonder if they were seeing things ! Three were in bed (it was 1.00 in the morning), two who had just come off watch were turning in, and the two on watch were doing odd jobs in the main buildings, filling up logs etc. Not a shot was fired on either side and no violence had to be used. They had quite a lot of arms about the place and two boxes of grenades open and ready for use. Their best weapon was an Oerlikon cannon shell gun, but we couldn't bring the weapons back with us as, with 19 men in, the landing craft was already pretty low in the water, so we dumped all their arms in the sea. We were under strict instructions not to interfere with or damage the light or its mechanism, but were allowed to smash up the wireless transmitter with which they sent all their naval messages, etc. This we did effectively !

" Re-embarkation was accomplished in the same manner and was without mishap except for me. I was left as last man, and so, of course, had no one to hold the boat in for me and no rope to slide down into it. I had to swim about 20 feet out to the boat, which, as soon as the tension came off the bowline was swirled back from the rocks by the swell, and I crocked my ankle whilst sliding down the rock into the water—my leg got doubled underneath somehow. However, it is nothing really and should be strong again in a week or ten days. The run home was uneventful, although with a rising wind and sea it was very wet, and we were back home by 4 a.m. ! Everyone is very pleased about the job—Chief of Combined Operations sent us a personal wire—and the prisoners are evidently talking quite well.

" Portsmouth has just informed us that Cherbourg was frantically calling up the Casquets all day yesterday and until midnight last night, and also asking all other stations if they had had any signals from the Casquets ! !

" By the way, Sark light was on ! Showing a red flash every 15 seconds. I should like to land on Sark again sometime.

" Don't tell the others about this, Dad. I tell you because if it should happen that one time I get left behind on one of these parties and so am out of action for the rest of the war, I should like you to feel that I'd had my share of the fun, and that it wasn't entirely a wasted effort. In fact, that there was a credit balance on our side, which, after all, is the main thing!"

In that letter Geoffrey didn't make much of the injury to his leg, but actually the bottom of the tibia was fractured. But despite the broken bone he was away on another raid two or three nights later. He wrote: "We were out again the other night (Monday) but it was a small and very unobtrusive party whose mission was purely a reconnaissance with a very particular end in view. No one was met, and I am quite sure no one on the other side ever knew we had been. It was in the same district as the previous one in which we robbed the nest and removed the seven eggs! By the way, these 'eggs' have 'hatched' very nicely and produced a great deal of extremely useful information.

"The other night's party was completely successful and we got all the information we wanted. I was unable to go ashore, of course, because of my ankle, but I navigated the party, and, from that point of view, it was by far the most interesting of anything we have yet done. It was great fun, as there was quite an element of cheek involved!

"Thank you for your prayers, Dad. And Mummy's too. I know they are a great help, and many of us pray very earnestly for the success of these parties and for the whole future of this type of operation, which I am convinced can play a real part in winning the war if taken up on an effective scale. When you pray don't just pray for our safety, but also pray for our success and our cause, and for one of the greatest things our little unit may help to achieve—the building up of morale in our own forces. When you pray for me, pray for courage and steadfastness and for my team spirit and loyalty to the other chaps on the job.

"I think we set out on these excursions very much in the spirit of Cromwell's injunction—'Put your trust in God, and keep your powder dry'! We'll do everything humanly possible to make them successful, and after that, we'll put our trust in God, and in our belief in the righteousness of what we are striving for and in our cause.

" The ' battle of Whitehall ' is, of course, now going a lot better. Never was the old adage ' Nothing succeeds like success ' more apparent, and our few small successes have helped enormously in London. In fact, people now are only too willing to give us what we ask. Gus has had several interviews with Mountbatten, and he has written us a personal letter of congratulation and encouragement."

Amongst the gallant band of the Commandos under training with Gus and Geoff on these night raids across the Channel was the strapping fair-haired Dane, Andy Lassen, previously mentioned in this story. Amongst other weapons he was a crack shot with a bow and arrow and would challenge anyone armed with a pistol against a target at 25 yards, and was known to some as the Robin Hood Commando. Gus soon realised the possibility of this archery and suggested to the War Office that steel bows and arrows be used on their night raids for the silent disposal of enemy sentries. Their use, however, was barred on the grounds of the arrow being an inhuman weapon—such is the anomaly of modern warfare that the traditional weapon of Crecy and Agincourt should be prohibited whilst resource is permitted to such horrors as rockets and atomic bombs.

Andy was recommended for a Commission by Gus and later for an M.C. by Geoffrey for the superb courage and qualities of leadership which he displayed. He was later to become Major Anders F. E. V. Lassen, V.C., M.C. and two Bars, and famous for his raiding exploits in Greece, Crete and Italy, falling mortally wounded in the action for which he was posthumously awarded the Victoria Cross.

About this date the *Tirpitz* was lying in a Norwegian fjord and constituted the greatest threat to British shipping. At a much later date we learned that Gus and

Geoff had submitted plans for a two-man submarine to be propelled by the two of them sitting, with a leg on either side of the craft, and pedalling as on a tricycle. The two were to be encased in diving suits of special design. This boat, which could be submerged, was to be launched from a submarine as near the fjord as possible and then propelled forward with the heads only of the two operators above the water, until when near the battleship the craft would be submerged, the diving suits brought into operation and sticky bombs placed on the bottom of the *Tirpitz* when it was contacted. It was claimed that this method would be silent and attract no attention. At first the ' powers that be ' blessed the plan and provided funds for the experiments. Later the *Tirpitz* moved its quarters and took up a position in another fjord where the speed of the outrunning current was greater than could be overcome by the power of the two ' cyclists.' This plan was then officially abandoned, but, as is well known, midget submarines, operated by the Royal Navy, later heroically succeeded in severely damaging the ship.

On one of their night raids on the French coast, Gus was advised that it would be safer to blacken their faces. He indignantly refused, retorting " If I am to die on one of these parties I'll die looking like an Englishman and not like a damned nigger "—a typical ' Gus ' remark for he was a very ' pukka ' soldier despite his informality.

At this time Gus and Geoff were very concerned about the " spirit of the Army " and the retreats in Greece, Crete and North Africa, and the disasters in Malaya and Singapore. They went so far as to write a paper conjointly on " Discipline and Morale " and sent it to the Army Command. Geoff sent home a copy for criticism, in reply to which he wrote : " On our weekend together we didn't discuss the paper on ' Discipline and Morale ' and the letter that you wrote to me commenting on it. The omission was purposeful on my part as I wanted to ' chew ' things over in my mind some more, particularly in the light of some of your comments.

" Your real criticism is that we are generalising too severely on the lack of spirit in the Forces. I think that perhaps the mistake there was that our argument was not put as well as it might have been in that it did not attempt to give concrete examples, nor did it suggest a further reason for our many defeats which has since occurred to me.

" Thinking things over after what you wrote, I think that perhaps our contention of ' lack of spirit' is neither fair nor true. I think it is more like ' lack of experience.' And I think that this can be explained. You see, in the last war, there was so much of a war atmosphere about and so more opportunity for men to become acclimatised to war before they were actually fully confronted with it.   Men were trained initially in England and then sent out to France, probably to some forward point behind the lines. Out there, there was a real war atmosphere—wounded men coming back, ammunition going up and being used, and perhaps an occasional long-range shell in their midst that caused casualties. And they began to learn what war really meant and their nerves hardened up to it.   And then later they went up into a quiet portion of the front line, where they only got a few shells a day, and the hardening process advanced another stage.   And so it went on until they were toughened and became seasoned troops that would hold together and not break in the very hottest of positions.   But to-day it is so very different.   We hold defensive positions in comfortable, almost peace-time conditions, day in day out, with no real war atmosphere, until suddenly the whole hell of modern blitz warfare bursts in a few hours, straight in one lightning jump from peace-time living to the most terrifying of conditions conceivable, and it's not surprising that we often crack up and fall back on rearward defensive positions, because nerves just aren't tuned up to it—we've never seen a man killed before—or heard the whine and crunch of a shell and the whistle of a bullet.

"And that is why we are pushing for a more aggressive policy—the only way we ourselves can push for it is to push for a really whole-heartedly adopted policy of small scale raiding, for thus can a large number of men get at least a taste of action, a ' baptism of fire,' and I'm sure it can make a real difference when the real thing comes along. Every single little operation you go on helps. Every time you get that tight feeling round your heart and the empty feeling in your tummy, you are mentally and nervously tougher than the time before and so are better fitted for real continuous military action.

" Remember too, Dad, that paper was written about the Army only. I agree that the record of the Air Force and the Navy and the Merchant Service in this war has been as fine as anything in English tradition. This, too, also supports the new argument that it is not ' spirit ' that is missing in the Army but ' experience.' For the Air Force and the Navy are more or less on active service all the time and therefore are continually tuned up and hardened to it. Also there is no lack of spirit in individuals in the Army to whom you talk. Every individual wants action and 95 per cent. would volunteer for almost anything you ask. And our Army record in offensive actions, such as Dieppe and St. Nazaire, has been good as regards the spirit in which our men have fought.

" No, it is not spirit we are lacking, but experience.

" I am afraid I have put my arguments very badly, but what do you think of all this ?

" Your other point was that ' adventure ' is not a sufficient ' gospel ' in itself. I completely agree, and the paper was certainly not intended to represent it as such. I also agree that our inspiration and drive must be founded on something infinitely deeper and more permanent than a mere love and genius for adventure, must have its roots in religious belief itself, and the knowledge of the essentials of good as distinguished from evil, the knowledge of the righteousness of our cause, the real value of liberty, and a host of other things that make life worth while and worth living, but I do believe we can make an approach to these things through appealing to the Englishman's inherent love of adventure and his genius for adventurous action. The Army to-day has no ' gospel,' no inspiration and drive, but, through adventurous action, I believe that the Gospel for which we are fighting can be evolved. Because it must grow in men—I don't believe you can educate men to have an inspiration by talking to them.

"And finally, remember that that paper was written as an argument—a piece of propaganda, if you like— for the policy of small-scale raiding, and so its arguments were to some extent used to this end! If it had been an essay on discipline and morale it would perhaps have been put slightly differently, although its matter would have been the same.

" Well, I think I've burbled on long enough. You must be tired of reading it! God bless, Dad. Very much love, Geoff."

A few nights later, on September 12th, 1942, the extraordinary run of immunity which had characterised all their raids came to a tragic close. Owing to the broken bone Geoffrey was still unable to walk except with support. Nevertheless, he went with Major Gustavus March-Phillipps, D.S.O., M.B.E., Captain Graham Hayes, M.C., and others on a raid in a motor boat as Navigating Officer, in which capacity he had by now acquired considerable skill. The Admiralty had given him the exceptional honour for a military man of navigating their craft. The party reached their desired spot in pitch darkness near the Cherbourg peninsula, cut off their two principal engines to avoid noise and crept into the bay on their small silent auxiliary engine. Lying off the coast, Major March-Phillipps (Gus), Captain Hayes (Graham) and nine others got into the landing boat. Geoffrey, being unable to walk, was unable to go, and remained in the motor boat off shore.

The party landed, pulled the wooden landing boat a little way up the beach, and set off for their objective a little way inland. This they successfully reached but found it to be more heavily guarded than they had anticipated and so Gus decided not to attack then but to return at a later date with a larger raiding party.

He therefore led the party back towards the beach. They were only about two hundred yards from their boat when they heard a small patrol approaching. Gus decided to ambush these Germans and attempt to capture a prisoner to bring back to England for interrogation. He therefore disposed his men alongside the path and waited. The German patrol walked straight into the trap but the fight which developed was so fierce that all seven of the enemy were killed. When Gus was searching the dead for maps and other useful documents, another and much larger German patrol was heard running towards them, having been attracted by the sound of firing. To attempt to stay and fight these superior forces was hopeless and so Gus's party ran for their boat, launched it and paddled away from the beach. They had only got about a hundred yards out when the pursuing Germans reached the shore and sent up a Verey light. This illuminated the small wooden boat trying to escape seawards and immediately a hail of fire was turned upon it. Gus and three others were killed, and the rest, some of them wounded, were flung into the water as the boat sank.

Meanwhile, Geoff, having no other boat in which to land, and unable to get his ship close in to the shore because of the shallow water, and unable by reason of his broken ankle to walk in any case, could do nothing to help. He could see no definite target at which to fire but brought his ship in as close as possible and heard the firing gradually die down. He heard a voice, believed to be Graham's, call out that all was lost and asking him to go away and save his ship. Nevertheless, he hung on, trying to find him and any other survivors up and down the coast, calling by whistle and showing a signal light, hoping to pick someone up. The motor boat was under constant gunfire from the shore and one of her two main engines was hit and put out of action. With the approach of day Geoffrey had no option but to save his craft. It was now no longer possible to get back by creeping along the mine-free channel near the coast as this was dominated by heavy coastal batteries. As daylight came he was therefore compelled to make straight back for home on a direct course through the minefields, and accomplished the run without mishap, being escorted into Portsmouth by Spitfires sent out to meet his ship and keep off enemy attack.

At a much later date it was possible to piece together the story of what happened to the survivors of the raiding party when their boat sank.

Graham Hayes, being a very strong swimmer and unwounded, managed to swim along the coast and was eventually washed ashore some way from the scene of the attack. After a night in a hayloft he entrusted himself to a friendly farmer who looked after him well for some time. He was then given food, clothes and money and passed on, by the " underground " to Paris, where he was given refuge in a Frenchman's home and, passing off as a deaf and dumb nephew, openly visited the cinema and football matches. He decided to make a bid to get home. He was provided with a fake *carte d'identité* and a patriot—afterwards murdered for his work— guided him safely over the Spanish border. A message of this good news was conveyed to Mr. and Mrs. Hayes.

Then tragedy stepped in. The Spanish authorities handed Graham over to the Germans who placed him in Fresnes prison, Paris, in solitary confinement. He was kept there for nine months until July 13th, 1943, when he was shot by the Germans under circumstances which have not yet been ascertained.

Of the others, Lord Howard was badly wounded in the leg and only just managed to struggle ashore where he was captured.

André Desgrange was also captured, imprisoned, questioned under duress, and shackled so that he could only eat from a trough direct by his mouth. He escaped to Spain, was imprisoned there and treated so badly that although phenomenally strong physically he fainted four times under the treatment. He escaped once again, got back to England, and in three to four weeks returned to France as an agent.

Two others managed to get ashore unseen by the Germans and were at large for four days before being captured.

Sergeant-major Tom Winter attempted to swim out to Geoffrey's ship and was within fifty yards of it, though not observed by those on board, when the ship received a direct hit from a gun on the shore and had to move out to sea. He was by then almost exhausted but just managed to get back to the beach where a German attempted to shoot him as he lay gasping for breath at the water's edge. Luckily the shot missed and he was taken prisoner. He then had to watch whilst the Germans proceeded to ' beat up ' one of the party who had just struggled ashore. Although this man was a prisoner, they continued to hit him with stick grenades until he received such fearful injuries that he almost succumbed. He was later taken to a German hospital where he was interned, well treated, skilfully operated upon and his life saved ; but he still suffers serious disablement.

Winter eventually found himself in a prison camp in Poland. After many months he found a way of getting in and out of the camp, and such was his courage that instead of attempting to escape he went out by night, contacted the " underground " and for many weeks trained Polish saboteurs in the use of explosives—returning to the camp each time by dawn. The Germans eventually suspected him of this and he was sentenced to ten years' solitary confinement. When the Russians began to advance on the Eastern front he was forced, along with hundreds of other prisoners, to march westwards, but eventually escaped and reached our lines.

Gus wrote a poem in Africa which might well be regarded as his own noble epitaph. It ran :—

1941

If I must die in this great war
When so much seems in vain,
And man in huge unthinking hordes
Is slain as sheep are slain,
But with less thought ; then do I seek
One last good grace to gain.

Let me die, Oh Lord, as I learned to live
When the world seemed young and gay,
And ' Honour Bright ' was a phrase they used
That they do not use to-day
And faith was something alive and warm
When we gathered round to pray.

Let me be simple and sure once more,
Oh Lord, if I must die,
Let the mad unreason of reasoned doubt,
Unreasoning, pass me by,
And the mass mind, and the mercenary,
And the everlasting ' why.'

Let me be brave and gay again,
Oh Lord, when my time is near,
Let the good in me rise up and break
The stranglehold of fear ;
Say that I die for Thee and the King,
And what I hold most dear.

This raid took place in the same neighbourhood that later became famous as one of the landing places of the Allied Forces when the invasion of Europe took place. One wonders whether the purpose of the raid was to secure information to help form the plans which led up to that great occasion.

With Gus and Graham both gone, Geoff had lost two of his best friends in the one night and he felt it badly. Despite the fact that he was advised to remain in bed to rest his foot he felt it his duty to carry on and hobble about as best he could. He was now temporarily in command of the Small Scale Raiding Force and shortly after was promoted to the rank of Major—one of the youngest at that time in the British Army.

Within a month, despite the broken leg bone, he was raiding again, at a spot where once in happier times family holidays had been enjoyed. He wrote to his younger brother : " Last Saturday night really was fun. We spent over four hours there and had a really good browse round before we rang the bell and announced ourselves. It was so strange to see old familiar places again. Such as the tree under which you found half-a-crown ! Remember ? I recognised it immediately.

" Our enforced guest of the evening has proved to be a winner ! And I saw a report yesterday saying that he was considered to be the most useful prisoner obtained by anyone up to date. He has proved very chatty and nothing is too much trouble for him to describe in detail.

" Yesterday was a very thrilling day—partly spent at the House—in the Prime Minister's private room. He unexpectedly congratulated me. The C.I.G.S. shook hands and said ' It was a very good show ! ' That was General Sir Alan Brooke, of course. General Sir Ronald Adam was also present (as were Pound, Anthony Eden, and quite a few other well-known people) and he said almost exactly the same thing. . . . The Chief of Staff has directed the Chief of Combined Operations to make Small Scale Raiding a major part

- - - - - - - - - - - - - - -

PLATE XIII

RAIDING ON THE ENEMY'S CHANNEL COAST

This drawing by William McDowell appeared in *The Sphere* and depicted one of Geoffrey's most successful Channel raids. This is the type of boat used by him for crossing the Channel in the raids described in Chapter V. Landings were made in small wooden and other craft carried on the deck

By courtesy of the " Sphere " and " Illustrated Newspapers "

of his policy and has said that we are going to be given every assistance and facility ! Wouldn't Gus have been thrilled ! That is the type of recognition for which he was always working."

Geoff's own brief description, at the beginning of this letter, of a raid carried out by a party under his command, gives but little idea of the success of this particular operation.

His planning of it began some weeks before the event when he was at home on a week-end's leave. We couldn't, at that time, understand why he was so keen to see a cinema film which we had taken on a family holiday in the Channel Islands some years before the war. But after the raid was announced in the papers, we realised that he had been refreshing his memory of one of the islands so that he could land with his men by night and lead them with sureness and certainty across the same beaches and up the same cliffs as he played upon as a boy.

By this stage of his career Geoffrey had gained so much experience of navigating motor gun-boats close in-shore, that he was usually made responsible by the Admiralty for all the navigation required on these raiding expeditions, because the naval officers who commanded the boats were very rarely experienced in navigating for hours on end amongst the reefs and tidal races which abound all round the Normandy coast and Channel Islands.

On the night of this particular raid Geoff chose to land on one of the islands' cliffs instead of on a beach because of the probability of the latter being mined. He left the gunboat about three hundred yards out from the cliff with orders to her commander that if the

---

Plate XIV

LANDING FOR THE PANTELLARIA
RECONNAISSANCE

J

raiding party had not returned in two hours' time, he was to abandon them and return to England as it would mean they had been captured.

The actual landing was made in a special wooden craft which was left at the bottom of the cliff with one man on guard.

As Geoff reached the top of the cliff after a stiff climb, and cautiously peered over the edge, he was horrified to see the vague silhouettes of a number of German soldiers about fifty yards away. He waited for some minutes in the hope that they would move on and then decided that here was an ideal opportunity to eliminate a complete German patrol and probably get a few prisoners as well. He therefore crawled stealthily towards the enemy and when he had so shortened the range that it was impossible for his men to miss, he prepared to give the order to fire. Then a doubt crossed his mind. None of the figures ahead of him had moved since he first saw them, nor had they made a sound. He decided to investigate and crawled nearer and nearer. Then to their amazement his men heard him chuckle, stand up and call them forward. They found him examining a row of perfectly dressed dummies used by the island garrison for target practice !

The raiding party had landed on a deserted part of the island about a mile from where the barracks was known to be and so they now advanced cautiously through the thick scrub. After a while they came to a house standing by itself and apparently deserted. Geoff decided to break in and search it. One of them forced a French window on the ground floor and they burst in with weapons at the ready. There was nobody in the downstairs rooms but as Geoff flung open a door on the first floor he was amazed to find an old lady fast asleep in bed ! On being awakened she was naturally terrified to find her room full of tough looking men with knives and pistols, but, discovering them to be British, soon recovered and, anxious to be of assistance, came downstairs. It transpired that she was English but had lived on the island from childhood. Geoff posted sentries outside the house, sent a man back the way they had come to tell the gunboat commander not to leave after two hours but to wait for their return, and then proceeded to chat with the old lady, seeking information. For about two hours she described in detail every German strongpoint on the island, the types of guns that were mounted, the number of troops in the garrison, when they were relieved, the state of their morale and in fact everything that Geoff calculated would be useful for the Allies to know if ever they decided to try and recapture the Channel Islands. He also obtained samples of the bread and other food issued as rations by the Germans so that an estimate could be made by the Ministry of Economic Warfare as to the effectiveness of the Allied blockade.

Other useful evidence obtained from her were copies of the island newspaper and also some proclamations issued by the Germans giving details of the proposed deportation of Channel Islanders to concentration camps on the mainland. This information was the first to be received by the British Government of the impending deportation, and hence was of very great importance.

Two days after the raid, every national newspaper in England carried reports and copies of this proclamation.

Having obtained all the information he could from the lady, Geoff offered to bring her back to England with him, but she refused to leave her home and possessions, and asked him to let her relatives in this country know that she was alive and well.

Geoff now decided that they must obtain a German prisoner at all costs in order that the old lady's information could be corroborated and amplified.

Time was running short and so he decided on a bold plan—to creep up to the German barracks, enter one of the outer huts, and take prisoner anybody in it. To get to the huts the raiding party passed through the grounds of the very hotel in which the family had stayed ten years before, and as Geoff said in his own letter, he was even able to recognise a large yew tree under which his younger brother had found half-a-crown during that carefree holiday.

Geoff cautiously opened the door of the hut he had selected, his men rushed in and soon five sleepy Germans were being hurried away from the barracks with the points of Commando knives pricking their backs. The party were only just clear of the houses in the village when they were spotted. A German patrol opened fire on them and in the ensuing confusion two of the German prisoners were killed and two escaped. None of Geoff's men were hit and they succeeded in getting back to the landing craft and out to the gunboat with their one remaining prisoner. They then found out that the man they had sent back to tell the M.G.B. commander not to leave, had got lost in the scrub, and had only reached him a few minutes before the main party, who by that time had been away for more than four hours. The naval officer had not left after two hours because he couldn't bring himself to believe that the party had all been captured or killed, and so decided to wait until the approach of daylight forced him to go. He therefore fixed himself a zero hour at which, come what may, he had to leave, and Geoff and his party finally reached the M.G.B. only five minutes before that time, just as he was giving the orders to start the engines.

The prisoner obtained on this raid supplied all the information that was required, and the great importance that was attached to the operation as a whole can be gathered from the last few paragraphs of Geoff's own letter in which he describes meeting the Prime Minister and other War Chiefs on the following day.

It is interesting to record that of this raiding party of about ten men, five were officers. They were Major Geoffrey Appleyard, Captain Colin Ogden-Smith, Captain Dudgeon, Captain Pinkney and Lt. (later Major) Andy Lassen. During the war three of these between them won one Victoria Cross, one Distinguished Service Order and six Military Crosses, but their magnificent achievement is overshadowed by the tragic fact that not one of the five survived to enjoy the Peace for which they all fought so gallantly.

Following that raid, in one of his speeches, Churchill said " The British Commando Raids at different points along this enormous coast, although so far only the fore-runner of what is to come, inspire the author of so many crimes and miseries with a lively anxiety. There comes out from the sea from time to time a hand of steel which plucks the German sentries from their posts with growing efficiency."

About this time Geoffrey wrote to the owner of the old Elizabethan Manor which was their base of operations : " I did so much appreciate the letter you wrote me some time ago, shortly after we lost Gus March-Phillipps.

· " His death was a tremendous blow to me, as you imagined. Gus meant a very great deal to me and he was my closest personal friend. We had been together for over two years and the occasion when he was killed was the one and only occasion in all that time that we were not actually alongside each other in every ' party.' On that occasion I had broken my ankle about a week previously, and so was unable actually to land, although I was with them up to the moment they landed.

" I have been wanting to tell you how much we appreciate the Manor—it has proved an ideal house in every way and to this unit a real home of which we have grown very fond. There is such a quiet and peace-ful atmosphere about the house and gardens, and often, after a night raid, coming back in the first light next morning, tired and often rather strung-up and on edge, it has been a real relief and relaxation to get back to such a lovely place. I know that Gus felt this very strongly—he often remarked on it to me—and I think the atmosphere of this house has, in an appreciable way, contributed to the making of what has been regarded in the high places, up to date, as a very successful little show. We have a grand crowd of men here and they have universally respected the privilege of living in this house. I don't think you would be disappointed if you could see the house now—it is kept beautifully clean, and, although sparsely furnished, is very comfortable."

Considerable expansion of the Small Scale Raiding Force was decided upon. Additional bases were formed in Dorset, Devon and Cornwall, and Lt.-Col. " Bill " Stirling was given command of the larger force with Geoff (a Major) second in command and chiefly responsible for leading active operations in the " field " —otherwise across the water.

By the beginning of November Geoffrey's leg, on which he had insisted on hobbling about, came to the notice of H.Q. at the War Office, and he was ordered into Millbank Hospital, where he was given the option of lying in bed for a month or having the leg in plaster from the tip of the toes to the knee and a metal stirrup under the heel along with a crutch. Quoting his letter of 5/11/42 : " I can get along at about two knots with a sort of bonkety-bonk action. I feel to have been made rather a fool. I went up the steps of the hospital at a run and came down two hours later a cripple and on crutches." Better news was that the injury persuaded him now to take some leave. Arrived home, his friends and neighbours at Linton and Wetherby desired to honour him on his award of the Military Cross and later the Bar thereto. At a meeting in the Wetherby Town Hall, on behalf of the Wetherby and Linton Services Welfare Committee, Mr. Hayes (father of Graham) handed him a silver salver bearing this inscription :—

> *Presented to Major J. G. Appleyard, M.C., by the people of Wetherby and Linton in grateful recognition of bravery and services in the World War in defence of those good and lovely things that go to make life worth living.*

The local paper reported : " In returning thanks, Major Appleyard said he would value the gift all his life. Though an unworthy recipient, he felt it was a symbol of the constant prayer and thought that the people of the two parishes had for all who were in the Services, and he was the fortunate one to receive the gift on behalf of every member from Linton and Wetherby. A number of others should be standing on that platform instead of himself, and one of them was Graham Hayes, second son of Mr. Hayes, reported missing two months ago. He was one of his greatest friends, and he had known him for fifteen years. During the last year they had been in the same unit together. Graham had always done a grand job and was absolutely reliable in any situation. Graham had been awarded the Military Cross recently. They had served together under the same Commanding Officer, a born leader, who would lead his men into any situation and one in whom the men had the utmost confidence. Like other great leaders to-day, he was a man who knew the power of God. He was killed quite recently. He stood for all those things for which the Nation was fighting. Major Appleyard read one of the Commanding Officer's poems." (This poem was the one commencing " If I must die in this great war," previously quoted on page 127.)

The leader writer of the paper made the meeting his subject that week. Here is an extract : " Mr. Hayes, whose own son has been missing for two months after conspicuous service to his country, for which he has been awarded the M.C., paid a tribute to Major Appleyard, which will be one of that officer's most precious memories throughout his life. After Mr. Hayes's truly great speech there came a reply by Major Appleyard such as enriches our national life. It would thrill all who heard it, and make them proud that they were privileged to count the Major as ' one of their very own.' The speech should be preserved in Wetherby's archives as the very essence of our conception of English character at its highest and best. We would say of Major Appleyard, as he said of that gallant leader of his who gave his life for his country, that he stands for all those things for which the nation is fighting. May all who heard the two speeches and all who read them resolve that they also will do everything in their power (and here we quote the inscription on the gift) ' in defence of those good and lovely things that go to make life worth living.' "

A big surprise awaited Geoffrey in regard to his cross-Channel raids for in December the *London Gazette* announced :—

War Office,

15th December, 1942.

The King has been graciously pleased to approve the following award in recognition of gallant and distinguished services in the field :—

The Distinguished Service Order.

Lieutenant (temporary Captain) (acting Major) John Geoffrey Appleyard, M.C. (86639), Royal Army Service Corps (attached a Special Service Brigade).

Lord Louis Mountbatten, Chief of Combined Operations, wrote personal congratulations as follows :—

19th December, 1942.

Dear Appleyard,

I was so very pleased to see that you had been awarded the D.S.O. and send you my heartiest congratulations. It was a very well deserved award and you have played a most important part in the execution of all the small raids which have been carried out by the Small Scale Raiding Force.

I hope that opportunity and good luck will give you every chance of achieving still further successes in carrying out this type of operation, and I feel sure that the skill and initiative which you have shown in the past will continue to contribute towards the future successes of the Small Scale Raiding Force.

Again my heartiest congratulations.

Yours sincerely,

LOUIS MOUNTBATTEN.

To which Geoffrey replied :—

Dear Admiral,

Thank you very much for your personal letter C.P.828/A of the 19th. I was very pleased indeed to have it and greatly appreciate your having taken the time and trouble to write.

I feel strongly that the award merely emphasises the extreme good fortune that I have had in being able to serve in this branch of Combined Operations, and am very grateful for the exceptional opportunities for action that we have had in recent months ; opportunities, however, which I am afraid others would have put to considerably better advantage.

Thank you for your good wishes for the future of our small force. I speak for everyone in the S.S.R.F. when I say that we are all determined to do everything possible to increase the effectiveness and the scope of these raids, and to make them an increasing source of worry and annoyance to the enemy.

Yours sincerely,

GEOFFREY APPLEYARD.

Vice-Admiral The Lord Louis Mountbatten,
G.C.V.O., D.S.O., A.D.C.,
Combined Operations Headquarters,
1a Richmond Terrace,
Whitehall, S.W.1.

The General commanding the Special Service, Major-General C. McV. Gubbins, c.m.g., d.s.o., m.c., also wrote, addressing Geoffrey by his universal nickname :—

My dear Apple,

Many congratulations indeed on your very well-deserved D.S.O., of which I have only very recently heard. I am delighted for your sake, and that of your unit.

My best wishes for your success in 1943.

Yours sincerely,

COLIN GUBBINS.

The Investiture at the Palace was Geoff's third such ceremony in eleven months. King George paused during the proceedings to have conversation with Geoffrey and opened by saying " What, you here again, so soon." His Majesty asked questions about the raids of which he had very considerable knowledge.

We arranged, as on Geoffrey's two previous Investiture evenings, a little dinner celebration at the Mayfair. All the invited guests were present, except Geoff! Immediately after leaving the Palace at noon he had a call from Harwich from his friend, (the late) Lt.-Cmdr. Robert Hichens, d.s.o. and two Bars, d.s.c. and Bar, of the " little ships " fame, to arrange the details for an urgent raid they were planning together, and Geoff did not arrive back until midnight just as the party was breaking up. It was a case of " The Play without a Hamlet."

It may be interesting to quote the Royal Warrant which carried the appointment to be a Companion of the Distinguished Service Order, headed by the personal signature of His Majesty, the King.

GEORGE R.I.

𝕲𝖊𝖔𝖗𝖌𝖊 𝖙𝖍𝖊 𝕾𝖎𝖝𝖙𝖍 *by the Grace of God of Great Britain, Ireland and the British Dominions beyond the Seas, King, Defender of the Faith, Emperor of India, Sovereign of the Distinguished Service Order, to our Trusty and Well beloved*

John Geoffrey Appleyard

on whom has been conferred the Decoration of the Military Cross, Lieutenant (temporary Captain) (acting Major) in our Army

Greeting

WHEREAS We have thought fit to Nominate and Appoint you to be a Member of Our Distinguished Service Order We do by these Presents Grant unto you the Dignity of a Companion of Our said Order And we do hereby authorise you to Have, Hold and Enjoy the said Dignity as a Member of Our said Order, together with all and singular the Privileges thereunto belonging or appertaining.

Given at Our Court at St. James's under Our Sign Manual this Fifteenth day of December 1942 *in the Seventh Year of Our Reign.*

By THE SOVEREIGN'S COMMAND

P. J. Grigg

The Principal Secretary of State having the Department of War for the time being.

Lieutenant (temporary Captain) (acting Major) J. G. Appleyard, M.C., Royal Army Service Corps.

Geoffrey took part in seventeen raids in which landings were made on the enemy coast, as well as making repeated crossings of the Channel night after night before a landing could be effected. He often remarked he found it far harder to do his duty and abandon an attempt, due to adverse conditions such as fog, or swell, or wind, or engine trouble, or enemy being reported in the vicinity, than to press on and make his attack.

About this time of continuous raiding, carried out night after night, Geoffrey received two invitations, both of which he had the bad luck to be prevented from accepting owing to absence from his base of operations and the fact that he did not return and receive them until too late. The first was from Their Majesties, the King and Queen, and the Princesses, who invited fifty young British and fifty young American officers to the Palace for a Thanksgiving Day party, Geoffrey amongst the number. The second was to spend a week-end, along with two young V.C.s, at the Prime Minister's home at Chequers where Mr. Churchill's family were to be present.

CHAPTER VI

NORTH AFRICA—SPECIAL AIR SERVICE

EARLY IN 1943 a big change took place in the work allotted to Commando No. 62, the one in which Geoffrey operated. It was considered the raiding experience they had acquired on the French coast could be put to the greatest use in the North African campaign and that they should operate not only on land and sea, but also in the air. The 62 Commando on arrival in Africa became known as No. 1 Small Scale Raiding Force, B.N.A.F.

In March 1943 Geoffrey wrote : " The receipt of this letter will signify my safe arrival at our destination as it will probably travel back to the U.K. on this same ship after we have been landed. So far this trip has been entirely uneventful although with fairly rough seas especially for the first two days out. However, I was delighted to find that I was entirely unaffected by the movement of the ship and actually my appetite seemed to improve with deteriorating conditions— maybe because, owing to larger gaps in the ranks at the tables at meal times, food in the dining room became more plentiful. ' It's an ill wind . . . etc.' Actually the food has been good, not quite up to the luxury standard of that on my troopship of eighteen months ago, but we have had fresh fruit (oranges and dates) several times and quite a lot of eggs, so don't do badly !

" To-day we have suddenly sailed into summer ! I am sitting on the boat deck, in shirt sleeves, basking in hot sunshine and writing on my knee. It really is lovely to feel the sun on my skin again, but I suppose we shall get plenty of it in the near future.

" I have done quite a bit of reading on board, and have taken the opportunity of reading *The Years of Endurance* fully and carefully. It really is most excellent. I enjoyed it enormously and am now thirsting and searching for other similar books. We have done quite a lot of P.T. on board, and also several of us have made a point of running a mile daily on the promenade deck at a time when it is usually clear. It makes a very good track and we manage to do the mile in between 6 and 6½ minutes, which is quite a good time.

"Well, I expect my next letter will have considerably more news, but for the moment I seem to have told you all there is. I am very well and eagerly looking forward to the future, about which, of course, there is a great deal of speculation going on, but very little information ! My 'flu is completely better, and I have now had all the inoculations (including typhus). Vaccination did not take. Dearest love to you all. God bless. Geoffrey."

Another letter followed a few days later. " I am writing this on my knee sitting in the back of my 15 cwt. truck. We are right up in the hills and so we have pulled off the road early for the night, and shall be starting at first light in the morning in order to have the light for the rough and difficult roads. It is very damp and wet as it has rained all day, and there is drifting mist about, and so we shall probably sleep on the floor of the truck instead of bivouacking on the ground as usual. We have just cooked our supper of sausages (tinned) and scrambled eggs and tea. Brownlie (my driver) did the sausages and I did the eggs ! Eggs are very plentiful and may be bought for 2-3 francs each (i.e., 2½—3½d.) or bartered for the less attractive parts of the Army ration—e.g., biscuits ! For breakfast we shall again have sausage and egg, but both are very good, and it will be a long time before I tire of eggs ! The night is very still now and the clouds are clearing away—it seems very lonely up here (I hope there are no parachute guerillas about !) and the only sound is the distant croaking of frogs on a marsh. We are in a clearing in the scrub, with some very English looking grass under foot, and a few cork trees and olives, and then scrub. All around are the black humps of scrub covered hills.

" This is a very fascinating country. It really is absolutely beautiful and infinitely varied—at times almost desert, and then a few miles later one could be in England on the Downs, and then for miles it will be Mexico with dead flat plains stretching away to sudden scraggy bare rocky hills, and then suddenly one sees views of blue hills and valleys for all the world like Scotland. I really am immensely taken with what I have seen of both Tunisia and Algeria. They would be magnificent for a family touring holiday, and the roads are not at all bad in general as long as you stick to the few really main ones which are well surfaced and engineered. I have been travelling about a good lot making contacts and getting things ' laid on,' and everything is going very well indeed. Very few snags, and everyone being most co-operative—that is the best of being in a theatre of war again—people cut the cackle and get down to it and things move enormously quicker and more easily. Most of my travelling has been by road in either a 15 cwt. truck (when out for more than one day as it is big enough to sleep in under cover) or by jeep (incredible little cars !) when out on day runs. However, I have been doing a little flying—it is the only way when you have to go right back, and you can do in two hours what takes two days by road. Flying (with the Americans) is ridiculously easy, and is really more casual and simple than the average catching of a bus ! Train is out of the question—they take weeks ! I talked to some Americans the other day who had been in the same cattle trucks for seven days, and they still hadn't arrived !

" I am allowed to tell you the places I have visited so long as I don't mention locations or where I am at the time of writing. I have seen Oran, and visited Algiers, Constantine, Philippeville (lovely place), Bone, Tebessa, Souk El Arba, Souk El Khemis. The last two are in Tunisia, and that is about the lot that you will find on the map. Constantine is remarkable—built on both sides of a terrific gorge, and with many historic connections as Dad will know. Algiers must be a lovely place in peace-time, but now with empty shops and no food it is pretty miserable and I was glad to leave it after two days. The Germans and Italians (through their 'Armistice' Commissioners) have absolutely sucked this country dry in the last two years. There is nothing to buy whatsoever. Actually everyone has heaps of money, even the scruffiest Arab (presumably because the American Army has so much to throw about), but no one can buy anything. A twopenny packet of dry Army biscuits will buy you more eggs than a 10 franc note, and the other day a filthy old Arab implored me to take a 500 franc note (£2 10s.) for my duffle coat! He didn't get it! Of course, trafficking in Army goods is strictly forbidden, but it must be a great temptation to the lads with the prices that are offered for any old worn-out garment.

" Our base is in a most delightful place, right on the sea amongst the sand dunes and about ten miles from the nearest town. A really healthy spot (all in tents, of course) and in an excellent training area. We are making it our permanent base, rest camp, training, holding and stores depot. Wonderful surfing and great fun with the boats for training in surf work, etc., and the length

PLATE XV

GUS

Major GUSTAVUS MARCH-PHILLIPPS, D.S.O., M.B.E.

GEOFFREY

Major JOHN GEOFFREY APPLEYARD, D.S.O., M.C. and BAR, M.A.

GRAHAM

Captain GRAHAM HAYES, M.C.

When the sad news arrived of the loss on the same day of Geoffrey and Graham, though so far separated, J.G., a fellow officer, wrote :—

" It is wonderful to think of Geoffrey and Graham going together and joining Gus who has gone before ! What shining examples those three are in their different ways ! "

and height of the surf is about Newquay standard.
Actually the temperature of the water at present is
much the same as north Cornwall in summer—pretty
cold in fact, but very invigorating, and you can stay in
half an hour or so if surfing. I have bathed every day
so far before breakfast whilst at the Base.

" The weather is very variable, some absolutely
heavenly days, like the very best days of an English
summer, and of a perfect temperature, so that we are
all already very brown about face and hands, and then
there are other days like to-day wet and dull with low
driving clouds. Nights are cold—the other night when
sleeping out there was quite a sharp frost (my Icelandic
sleeping bag still proved adequate and sufficient even
though lying on the bare ground and a groundsheet).
My duffle coat is a godsend—worn a great deal and
really much more use than a greatcoat or British warm,
both of which would have been very soon ruined as
there is an awful lot of mud about still.

" Food is good—it consists solely of Army rations
except for local eggs and fruit (oranges, tangerines,
dates and figs, all of which are plentiful). There are
virtually no restaurants or cafés anywhere in the country
where you can get a meal except black market ones if
you know them. I tried in the best restaurant in
Algiers to get a meal—it consisted of very thin poor soup,
second course, plain rice—third course, boiled turnips—
fourth course, an orange. That was all I could get, no
fish or meat at all. But the Army rations (mainly
tinned meat, etc.) are very good and plentiful. I am
extremely well and feel very invigorated and refreshed
by this climate and the new experience of being out here.

"Also, of course, I am continually being thrilled and
delighted with this country. It really is very fascinating.
As regards natural life, there are a lot of birds, some
very English—swallows, martins, skylarks—and some
very foreign—vultures, hawks, eagles, storks (all
standing on their nests on one leg), etc. Flowers are
not really out yet, but there are quite a lot of small

K

spring wild flowers, mostly very small, but at times, looking across the ground, you get the most lovely ' patch' colour effects with the myriads of tiny little flowers—great yellow, brown, pink or purple patches cover the hillsides in places. But most lovely of all are masses of most gloriously scented wild narcissi that grow in swampy places, with a lovely sweet, ' heady' smell. Scorpions (yellow and black) abound in stony places and later there will be a lot of snakes, but we have only killed one in the camp to date. At night the jackals come and howl round the camp (a weird and ' chilling' sound), but I haven't seen any yet. There are also wild boar about.

" I expect to be back at our Base Camp to-morrow night, when I shall have been away for four days and three nights. I have not been on the road continuously all that time, but have been visiting various H.Q.s and formations, naval officers, and people, and fixing things up. However, one needs to travel with full rations and cook as you go along, as you cannot get a casual meal anywhere, and at night it is very much better to bivouac in the open air than in a filthy billet somewhere in a mud house in a town or village. Also hard lying is good training for the days to come.

"As regards prospects, they are good, and things will be very busy soon. I think now that I shall not be coming home again quite so soon as I indicated at first. We can do such a really useful job here and there is so much co-operation and keenness that we may get the whole party out if we can persuade London that to go whole hog for this end can be of much greater value. After all, this is where the war is now and is going to be in the future. If the home end is definitely to go on, then I shall return to run it, but will greatly have profited by this experience here. The job here will be the job that Jordan did. Ian will understand that if you say to him ' COJONES '! And I am dying to get on with it as it is what I have always hoped for."

The mystic reference to the job that Jordan did and " COJONES " being decoded refers to the activities in

For whom the Bell Tolls carried on by Jordan in the way of wrecking communications. " Cojones " is the hero's favourite and much used swear word. In the next letter which follows reference is made to the weight of the rucksack carried by each man—65 lbs. Of this 5 lbs. was food and 60 lbs. was mostly explosives.

There are no particulars in Geoffrey's letters of these sabotage expeditions. Lawrence of Arabia was one of his heroes as a boy. How little was it expected he would emulate his work !

We learned later that Geoffrey's H.Q. Camp, described above, was some miles east of Philippeville on the North African coast.

A long letter received at a much later date from his friend and fellow officer, Captain R. H. Bridgman-Evans, M.C., supplies additional details of the North African adventures to those described in Geoffrey's letters, and it may be interesting to quote therefrom as occasion arises.

Of the outward voyage and early days in Africa, Captain Bridgman-Evans writes : " It was some time in September 1942, just after Gus had been lost and Geoffrey promoted Major, that I was summoned to Whitehall. It was Geoffrey who interviewed me. I wish I could explain my feelings better—Geoffrey's eyes were so blue and looked so very straight at me—I know I had the feeling that he had summed me right up, and that if I had told a lie, he would have known it right away. When I walked out into Whitehall I was saying to myself ' I would follow that man anywhere '— I had only been with him fifteen minutes.

" From that time until we sailed for Africa in February 1943 I saw very little of him. What I did see I liked more and more. We sailed from the Clyde with Geoffrey in command of the party and myself second in command.

" During this trip I got to know Geoffrey quite well —we shared one small cabin. I was struck by the detailed knowledge he had of almost any subject, and his memory was remarkable. Many an hour he spent on deck at night, teaching us the stars.

"At Philippeville we formed the first Squadron. Geoffrey was in command and I was his second, and we got down to strenuous training right away. It was at this stage that he started teaching me how to plan operations. His detail in planning amazed me. Most of our operations were to be weight-carrying ones, and he had the Quartermaster weigh every item of equipment, even down to a box of matches. Every exercise was planned as an operation and carried out as such. I am convinced that his successes were due to this meticulous planning on which he insisted."

Writing on 26/3/43 Geoffrey said : " I think you would be surprised to see me now ! I am sitting, with a 5-days' growth of beard on my face, stark-naked in the sun, on a rock in the middle of a little stream, with my feet in the water, cooling off some of the blisters ! We are in a tiny little wadi in the midst of a cork forest and there are dense bushes of juniper, thorn, bamboo and broom all around, making this a most perfect little hide-out for the day. We got in here about 5 this morning after being on the move since 7-30 last night, and shall be off again as soon as darkness falls to-night. It's now just mid-day and I am having a glorious sun bathe whilst writing this before sleeping for another five hours this afternoon. I woke at about 11 a.m. and then had ' breakfast ' consisting of two biscuits, some cheese, six dates, two boiled sweets and a mess tin full of tea. We are all getting very adept at making smokeless fires for boiling water—the theory being that you use tiny and absolutely dry twigs and light it under a bush, so that what little smoke there is filters up through the foliage and is dissipated. The other five in the party are all just around me in tiny little clearings between the bushes—two are still sleeping, one is washing and the other two are lying down and talking quietly. Well, have you got the picture ?

"Actually it's easy enough to avoid being seen by British troops and formations, but it's the Arabs that are the trouble. They pop up everywhere, at all times, and seem to drive their wretched goats over every inch (accessible and inaccessible) of the country. However, I am prepared to bet two of my precious biscuits that we shall not be found here this time. It's a perfectly hidden spot, and I don't think even a goat and an Arab could push through the ring of those bushes we had to get through to get in here!

"I think this is quite the toughest thing physically I have ever done. We are each carrying 65 lbs. (sixty-five) packs (rucksacks) and if you want to know just how heavy that is, Ian, try it! This country is most incredibly difficult to move over and through, and the maps are abominable, so that one mile per hour is quite a good average speed. Heaven help the carto-grapher who made the map! Last night an apparently good track landed us up in the middle of a swamp from which we took two hours of plunging and forcing to extricate ourselves. If curses can kill, that man won't be alive now!

" Short interlude—there are 24 Fortresses escorted by 18 Lockheed Lightnings passing dead overhead, going E.N.E., Tunis or Bizerta, I suppose.

"We started this scheme last Monday and now, with only about fourteen more miles to go, should be back in camp just before dawn to-morrow. So far in our four nights' travel we have covered about forty miles as the crow flies, but you cannot measure distance in this country in miles, as in that time we must have climbed between 6,000 and 8,000 feet.

" I hope this isn't all boring you ? Actually with not having got any of your mail yet there is very little else to write about!

"As long as you have plenty of liquid—and luckily there is no shortage of that yet in this country—it is amazing how little food you do require (or even want) on a scheme of this sort. For example, we started off five days ago with a total weight of 5 lbs. of food consisting of biscuits, dates, boiled sweets, bully beef, cheese, a small tin of sardines, and tea, sugar and milk mixture. I still have at least half of it left.

" The weather seems to have improved this last week or so, and we have not had a single drop of rain for days. It is really lovely, and at the present moment the temperature is about that of a really warm English summer's day. Sitting with nothing on I am exactly the right temperature, and keep altering my position so as to get evenly sunburnt and not ' over-done.'

" Water, of course, is just drunk as you go along—sometimes from a mountain stream and sometimes from the middle of a stinking swamp, but one always chlorinates it. We have an excellent little sterilizing set each, and one chlorine tablet in a bottle of water, and then one ' Thio ' tablet to take the taste of the chlorine away, and then one can safely and pleasantly drink the very foulest water.

" I must say I still find this country very fascinating. There is so much variety of natural things—for instance, oak, ash, brambles and bracken alternate with cork, palm, cactus, orange and tangerine trees ; and herons, blackbirds, great tits and woodpeckers are all mixed up with stork, vultures, egrets, flamingoes, and eagles. I even heard a cuckoo the other day, and saw swallows and pied wagtails, going north presumably. I'll send my greetings with them ! Linton must be looking very lovely now and when you get this the daffies will be out and April will be with you. The first nests—and the dippers. Tea at Malham, and perhaps ham and eggs. I suppose I'll miss all that this year. Still there's a job to do here first, and then, perhaps, a year hence it will all be over.

"And now the Fortresses are coming back overhead—in ones and twos now, straggling. They've dropped a grim load somewhere.

" Margot would delight in the flowers out here, although I suppose they are not nearly at their best.

Our camp is full of wild lavender, growing everywhere, and my tent is carpeted with it. Well, for the present, au revoir. Dearest love to you all. As always, Geoffrey."

On another occasion they successfully raided one of the smaller islands immediately to the north of Bizerta.

His letter of 12/4/43 told of a strange mishap. " Dearest Dad, Mummy, Margot, Joyce and Ian, Cheers and again cheers ! Your first mail has arrived, consisting of three air mail letters, the very first word I have had since leaving home, and so a very great thrill. I read them over and over again.

" I had an extraordinary accident the other day and collected my first war scars, but very inconspicuous ones ! I now have a very neat ·45″ hole through my left shoulder (from back to front, I'm afraid), but collected it in a very unromantic way. Nothing at all to worry about as it didn't touch a thing—just in through the flesh, only just clipped the muscle and out again, but it makes quite a nice little hole. I was remarkably lucky actually—another half-inch to one side and it would have hit the bones and I would have been out of action for six months, whereas it is now, although only a week ago to-day, as good as new with only a little bit of sticking plaster over the hole where the bullet went in and another where it came out ! Also I was lucky in that at the split second that the chap fired I moved about a foot to one side, otherwise it would have gone slap through the middle of me !

" But here's the let-down—it was a Yank and not a Jerry bullet ! I was driving fast up the road and the bullet was apparently fired from the back of a big Yank lorry coming the other way just after we had passed it. I imagine there was a chap sitting in the back of it potting at the kilometre stones as they went past, when I suddenly flashed by and collected the bullet. Anyway, he didn't stop, and I didn't think of stopping him, being on my way to a ' party ' of ours at the time. I had a couple of live grenades in the back of my jeep, and when I heard the crack of the gun and felt a sharp burning pain in the shoulder I thought that one of my own bombs had gone off. It wasn't till we noticed the hole in the jeep dashboard that the bullet had gone through, and the size and cleanness of the hole in my shoulder, that we realised what had happened. I applied a shell dressing and sulphonamide powder immediately (we always carry them, also morphia) and drove on to the next unit with a M.O. He gave me an anti-tetanus stab, and directed me to the nearest hospital and even tried to get me to use an ambulance! However, I skipped the hospital as I knew that once I got there I'd miss our ' party ' and so drove on about three hours to our embarkation point and got hold of our own M.O.—Lt. Robb, R.A.M.C.—a parachute doctor and a really grand chap and first-class surgeon (he has just got the M.C. for performing 150 surgical operations in the field, under fire, with the parachute battalion). He had all his field stuff with him in readiness for our ' party ' and so strapped my shoulder up and dressed it beautifully and said I couldn't possibly do myself any harm by carrying on as long as the slight discomfort didn't worry me. So I was still able to lead my boys and we had a very amusing night's entertainment with a few I-ties! My left arm wasn't much use but it didn't really matter, and, in an emergency, with a little discomfort I could have used it as well as the other. Anyway, it's all making a perfect mend, and I've now got a dressing on that can stay there for a fortnight.

" You may not hear from me again for quite a bit. I expect to be out of touch from to-day for perhaps ten days or rather more, so don't worry. Will write immediately on return. Would you please send this letter on to Jenny and thank her very, very much for her letters. It was so lovely to have them, but I have hardly time to write another letter now. By the way, Jenny, I always carry my anthology with me in my rucksack and learn and read the poems in the long daylight hours! You may judge how completely healed my shoulder now is by the fact that I shall be carrying a 65 lbs. rucksack across it ! God bless you all. I shall be continually thinking of you all and praying for you in the days ahead."

This letter recalls Geoff's deep love of poetry and literature derived largely from his days at Bootham under the inspiration of Mr. Corder, the English master, and from the Sunday evenings when a few of the boys would sit round the fire in the study of their House-master, Leslie Gilbert, and listen whilst he read. Geoff had the faculty of being able to read a poem and recite it at once almost word perfect.

At Cambridge he was a member of the Shakespeare Society.

Amongst his favourite poems those dealing with nature and particularly mountains and birds held first place. Many are to be found in the anthology of *Poems of Lakeland* by Mrs. Ashley Abraham. Looking through his copy of this book marked as especial favourites are :—

A HILL

Only a hill : earth set a little higher
Above the face of earth . . .
. . . but all of life to me.

Geoffrey Winthrop Young.

*   *   *

I will go back to the hills again
That are sisters to the sea
. . . . . .
And their strength shall be my strength
And their joy my joy shall be.

Anon. (Journal of the Fell
and Rock Club).

*   *   *

OUTWARD BOUND

. . . The curlews faintly crying
'Mid the wastes of Cumberland.

Noel Oxland.

THE TREASURE OF HEIGHTS

Seek them, ye strong
The cold of morning and the mountain wind
. . . .
Who has the hills for friend
Has a God-speed to end.

GEOFFREY WINTHROP YOUNG.

*   *   *

WISE KINGS OF BORROWDALE

I dream that heaven is very like this land,
Mountains and lakes and rivers undecaying.

EDMUND CASSON.

*   *   *

As the marsh-hen secretly builds on the watery sod
Behold I will build me a nest on the greatness of God.

S. LANIER.

*   *   *

TO A WATERFOWL

There is a Power whose care
Teaches thy way along that pathless coast.

M. C. BRYANT.

*   *   *

One of his most treasured possessions was a beautiful leather backed pocket note-book in which his sister, Joyce (the " Jenny " of his letters) had copied out many of his favourite poems to form his own carefully chosen anthology. Often in lonely watches and desert surroundings, and in other times and places, did he find solace therein. Alas, it found a watery grave along with other personal possessions when, on the occasion of a night landing behind the enemy lines in Tunisia, later described, he and his patrol were ambushed and had to abandon all their rucksacks and impedimenta and swim for their lives to regain their boats.

"All's well, and we are all back here again in our pleasant base camp on the sand dunes very much sooner than expected. We have had an exciting and intensely interesting time since I last wrote four or five days ago, although on this occasion things didn't turn out quite as planned—hence the sudden return. One thing, though, that distresses me considerably is that I have lost (irretrievably, I'm afraid) my anthology, that Joyce wrote out and gave me, and to which I have often added. It makes me very sad to have lost it as it was a lovely collection and I shall miss it. However, my lucky mascot (Mummy's black cat drawing !) is still going strong, although he has had another long immersion in sea water and so his paint is beginning to run a bit more !

" My shoulder wound is really healing amazingly and is nearly quite normal now. I am doing full P.T. and training—except for the rough and tumble stuff— and the thing is drying up beautifully. I shall have the dressings off for good in a week or so, and meanwhile the only annoyance it causes is that I cannot go in the sea. When healed the two bullet holes will look like nothing more than bad vaccination marks.

" Summer seems to have really come now—the last month has been very patchy with wind and rain and terrific seas, and we have been wondering just when it would get really warm and settled. Apparently the good weather is several weeks overdue this year but everyone seems to think that it has now come to stay. Tropical kit has been drawn, and we are daily awaiting the general order to don it. The nights are still delightfully cool (often really cold, and one is glad of a roaring camp fire and a warm sleeping bag) and the days as hot as summer in the south of France. Here on the sand dunes there is always a cool breeze ; and mosquitoes, flies and sandflies haven't yet become annoying. Oranges and tangerines are about over, but there are still masses of dates and lemons and, of course, eggs ! We catch a lot of fish here—all with explosive I'm afraid—but to-night we are going to take out a boat and set half a dozen lobster pots we have bought from the local fishermen."

Geoffrey's reference in this letter to his "lucky mascot (Mummy's black cat drawing!)" was more than mere superstition. That black cat post card was one his mother had sketched in his school days and he had carried it through his school and college exams., and in all his ski-ing races and military adventures. So many memories surrounded that tattered post card that it had become to him an inspiration.

On 25/4/43 he wrote: "Happy Easter to you all! I have had a lovely Easter present to-day—eleven letters! Have been away from here for five days in Algiers and only returned late this evening. Life is really pretty hectic and there is an immense amount to do, now and in the days to come. Although I flew both ways to Algiers (and shall be flying again for two hours to-morrow morning) there never seems to be a moment to spare! I am beginning to think that the faster the pace the less (and not more, as you might think) time do you get! To-morrow's flight will be rather fun—it's a special place for me to do a ' look-see ' and I shall be escorted by Spitfires!! Beat that, Ian! After that I shall be away a few days on a little party, then back to Algiers, and then immediately flying to Malta. Later I expect to spend a good deal of time there, probably semi-permanently. Am very well and happy to have had such frequent and good news of you all at home. God bless and keep you all. All my love, Geoffrey."

Later we learned that the place of the ' look-see ' was La Galite island off the coast of Tunisia. The incident is more fully described later in Captain Bridgman-Evans's letter. Next week's letter read: "I am back in Algiers again, as I flew down a couple of days ago but expect to leave here to-morrow, flying to places considerably farther afield than I have been so far. Our little jaunt the other day (in a Walrus!) with an escort of six Spitfires was very amusing and quite exciting and we saw the ' Spits ' in action."

On the same day he wrote to his sister, Joyce, by now serving in the F.A.N.Y. and working under the Chief of the Special Service like himself: "I have

certainly seen a bit of this country now, having
motored and flown some thousands of miles over it.
Have seen quite a lot of Constantine which is rather a
fascinating place, built on both sides of a terrific gorge
like Cheddar, only much bigger. A very historical
place too. Also I know places in the war news such as
Cap Serrat, Sedjenane, Jebel Abiod (jebel or djebel is a
' hill '), etc., and southwards have been as far as Tebessa,
etc. I expect to broaden my boundaries very considerably in the very near future. Have also been about on
the sea quite a lot, in motor torpedo boats like those
we have at home, and feel to have been getting a good
deal of pretty useful experience. Am now again in
Algiers for a short time—it is not a pleasant place,
crowded and short of food, no restaurants or anything
(and no Hedy Lamarrs, but quite a few aspirant Hedys
among the local French girls, none of whom do I know !).
The flowers are very lovely — bougainvilia, roses,
carnations, cyclamen, lilies, etc., etc., in profusion. At
our Base Camp up country the flies and mosquitoes
are just now beginning to be troublesome. What will
they be like later ? Well, happy days, Jenny, and very
much love to you. Geoffrey."

On 26/5/43 he wrote : " My dearest Mother and
Dad, Margot, Joyce and Ian, I spent one night at the
base camp three nights ago, after an absence of over
two weeks and you can imagine how delighted I was
to find a large batch of letters waiting for me—five
from you, Mummy (the last dated 10/5/43 and the
others consecutive before that), four from Joyce, and
one each from Margot and Ian. It was lovely to have
so much news, and I consumed it eagerly—reading
your letters over and over again. When I get a batch
of mail like that I restrain my impatience to plunge
straight into them, long enough to open them all,
arrange them in progressive date sequence, and so get
a continuous story. I will answer them fully in my next
letter, as I have not got them available at the moment.

" There is no diminution in the interest (and excitement) of my job. I have been moving about a good

deal since I last wrote and must have flown many thousands of miles, flying being now more natural than motoring. Ian will be amused to hear that I had my own private ' Fortress ' for one trip and return three days later. I hope you have not worried at a gap of three weeks in my letters to you, but I hope my two cables sent on occasions when I was in Malta will have reassured you. I have really been extremely busy and living at an extraordinary speed ! Malta is a most interesting place—reminds me tremendously of Venice —or rather Valetta does, and the part round there, which is the only part I have seen. All one's voyaging is by water in ' dghaises,' pronounced ' diser,' and the quays and houses are very Venetian. It is an extraordinary and charming island—quite ' different.'

" Your descriptions of the garden at present sound lovely and make me feel quite homesick ! However, there is every chance that about August I shall hand over my job here to someone else, and will be returning home—in time for a little tennis before the season ends. That would be fun !

" Meanwhile, my very dearest love to all and each one of you. I am constantly praying for you and thinking of you all, and looking forward so much to the next time we are all home together. God bless you. My very dearest love, Geoffrey."

Captain Bridgman-Evans' letter gives more details of Geoffrey's activities in North Africa up to this date, as follows : " It was on the first operation, when we did a four-hours' night reconnaissance of the island of La Galite, that I discovered his great courage and coolness. On the way to the port from which we were to embark, Geoffrey was shot through the fleshy part of his shoulder, by an American shooting out of the back of his truck going in the opposite direction to Geoffrey's jeep. Most men I know would have stood down from the operation, but not so Geoffrey. He had it strapped up and insisted on going on. There were 350 Italians on the island. Geoffrey's intention was to land with forty men, secure the high central point, capture a prisoner and send him to the Italian C.O. with an ultimatum that unless he paraded all his troops without arms at a specified place by dawn, the town would be shelled both by the landing party and by naval craft. (Actually Geoffrey had no guns at all.) The plan fell through because heavy seas on the way to the island badly damaged one of the landing craft and only a small party could be put ashore, with a view to reconnaissance for a return visit.

"Some time after we had landed on the island, Geoffrey came back down the patrol to give me some instructions. He put his hand on my arm and I could feel it trembling from the pain of the wounded shoulder, yet his voice was as steady and as natural as it was on an exercise. I had heard people say ' Oh, he's hard, he doesn't know what fear is.' But I knew then that Geoffrey probably had more imagination than any of us. The control he exercised must have been terrific.

"A week or so later Geoffrey and I did a daylight air reconnaissance of this same island. The only available plane was an ' air-sea-rescue ' Walrus, so away we went with an escort of six Spitfires. Eighty-five knots was her speed and 100 ft. our altitude most of the way. As we drew near the island, I know I was keyed right up and so was the pilot, Geoffrey started talking over the intercom. pointing out how beautiful the island looked with the sun shining on it. He kept this up, directing the pilot at the same time. We made three runs the whole length of the isle. I could see the light A.A. fire hitting the water between us and the beach ; we were lower than the cliffs and they were firing down on us. The Spitfires were straffing the ground defences. Geoffrey never mentioned the A.A. fire till afterwards, he just continued talking about the landing possibilities of the beaches. He then asked the pilot to fly right over the top of the highest point, which was 1,200 feet. This the pilot did—I cannot say I enjoyed it—but Geoffrey wanted to be sure just what in the way of defences, if any, was on top.

" He was a great man for boats and no sea was too rough for him to try and get out the dorys we used on operations. I have seen him try three or four times to get one out through the breakers, only to be swamped or overturned time after time, but he invariably succeeded in the end. The men would always volunteer to go with him. He inspired confidence.

" One afternoon, I believe a Sunday, Geoffrey, Johnny Cochrane and myself, being the only ones in camp, decided to have a swim. The sea was very rough and the rollers were breaking about 150 yards out. Geoffrey suggested swimming out beyond them. I said ' Not for me.' We dived through a few breakers and then I looked back and found we were far further out than I thought. I called Geoffrey's attention to this, saying I was starting back. Going out had been easy but getting back—well, the breakers drove one right down and rolled one over and over, and just as one reached the surface another would do the same thing. I remember after three or four of these I screamed ' Geoffrey, I don't think I can make it.' Back came his dear calm voice, ' It's all right, Roy, don't struggle, just keep yourself afloat, tread water.' Each time I came up Geoffrey would encourage me. I believe it took us fifteen to twenty minutes to regain the beach. I could not stand when we eventually got ashore. I know that if it had not been for Geoffrey I should never have made it. All this time I never knew that he himself had been in trouble and that he believed he was going to be drowned. Fifteen minutes later, when we went into the Mess, Geoffrey's hand trembled so much he had to take both of them to lift his tea cup. He then said, ' I always wondered how it was strong swimmers drowned, now I know.'

" It was not long after this that Geoffrey and I with two patrols using two dorys tried to make a landing by night in Tunisia behind the enemy lines with a view to sabotage on the way to Mateur, sixty miles to the south, followed by a break back through the German line to regain our base. We were unfortunate enough to hit a sandbank about sixty yards from the beach over which the boats would not ride. Each man had a rucksack, with explosive weighing 60 to 65 lbs. on his back, even our weapons were waterproofed and packed in these. We had almost gained the beach wading up to our armpits, when a German patrol opened fire on us. Geoffrey was actually on the beach ; perfectly calm, he ordered all men to regain the boats, talking to us all the time, giving orders. Rucksacks had to be dumped in the water and each man had to swim to regain the boats. Not a man was lost."

The incident well illustrated a favourite parody of the motto on the S.A.S. regimental crest "WHO DARES WINS"—to which they added : "AND WHO DOES—SWIMS." The S.A.S. badge is depicted on the title page of this book. It symbolises the dagger of the Commandos and the upturned wings of those airborne troops whose duties include dropping by parachute behind the enemy lines.

Geoffrey's activities had evidently been closely watched from Combined Operations Headquarters in London for he received a letter from Major-General Charles Haydon, second in command to Admiral Lord Louis Mountbatten, reading :—

> *My dear Geoffrey,*   3/6/43.
>   *How are you ? I hear you are doing great things—which is what we all expect of you but always with the strict proviso that you go on being wise and of good, shrewd judgment as you have in the past. Please write when you can instead of maintaining a stony and uninformative silence.*
>   *I enclose a note from " you know who."*
>   *All good fortune and my very best wishes.*
>
>   *CHARLES HAYDON.*

The pace was getting more and more hectic and experiences more and more varied. In the following extract Geoffrey's reference to ' Bone ' refers to his first submarine trip.

L

"I am at the moment sitting on an airfield, having just got in from my fourth visit to Malta, and am waiting for a jeep, for which I have just telephoned, to arrive to take me back the 2½ hours' run to our Base Camp. This has been a varied, much travelled and very busy six weeks, and I am now hoping to spend a week or two at the Base. During the past six weeks I have only ' called ' at the Base Camp twice, each time for a few hours only, so all my recent mail has been in two batches—but what grand batches !

"Have had a good deal of excitement lately, but am expecting a quiet time for a few weeks now. You will have seen news items lately and heard them on the wireless, which I think you may have guessed concern us. And others that you will *not* have guessed concerned us ! We have done one or two things which I think have undoubtedly been of considerable value in the bigger picture, and a certain amount of satisfaction about them has been expressed in high quarters. It has been very interesting, and of great interest to me to see the very different problems and possibilities here, in this theatre of war, and against this enemy, rather than in the place (and against the enemy) that we were working in last summer and winter. I have been surprised to find that principles of war are not by any means religiously the same in both places.

"You remember the journey, lasting four weeks, on which I met an officer called Bone ? You will doubtless be surprised to know that I have now made four more similar journeys, all very much shorter, of course, the longest being a week, and the shortest four days. And so I now feel to be quite an ' old hand ' after five trips of that sort, and am almost thinking of asking for a transfer ! It is certainly a fascinating job, and I think it might have been just my vocation ! However, don't get alarmed—a transfer would be quite impossible !

"Here's a coincidence. Under these rather strange conditions (you can imagine them) and immediately prior to something that I expected to find rather exciting, I discovered in conversation with the commanding officer that we raced against each other in the visitors' hotel relay ski race at Zermatt in 1938, when I won that cigarette lighter. Peter Lunn was in the same race. Actually he had recognised me, but until that moment we had not been able to work out where and how we could have met. Wasn't it extraordinary, to meet again under those conditions, and compare them with our last encounter—midwinter, snow, frost, sunshine and friendly sport with Germans and Italians! It made one feel rather strange for a minute or two and very fed up with present form! I discovered, by the way, that Roxburgh (his name) also knows the Chief quite well.

" Flying has now become quite a matter of routine and has quickly lost all its thrill, except when one is passing over some place of particular interest. The other day I flew low over Tunis and Bizerta shortly after they fell, which was most interesting, but otherwise I have not visited those places. We have four times lately had private planes when it was a matter of moving a party quickly for some important job, and once I had a private Fortress all to myself to take me somewhere, wait four days, and bring me back again. A great thrill—they are wonderful planes, and about as safe as anything could be with that power and armament."

This letter gives but little idea of what Geoffrey had been doing on his flights and submarine sailings from Malta, and we never knew the whole story until one day in the spring of 1945 an officer came into the mess in Sussex where his younger brother, Captain Ian Appleyard, R.E.M.E., was located. Being introduced, he at once asked if Ian knew Major Geoffrey Appleyard and then said he had worked with him in North Africa and asked if we knew what he had been doing there, where his name had become quite " legendary." He told some of his achievements and among them gave the following account of the activities mentioned in the letter just quoted.

Geoffrey was personally requested by General Alexander to survey thoroughly the rocky island of Pantellaria, strongly held by 13,000 Italian troops and heavily fortified against all attack. He was to furnish such details as would enable the General to decide on the best methods of assault. On four separate occasions he was flown out to Malta and twice made separate excursions from there by submarine to survey Pantellaria.

A letter written by Lt. John Cochrane, an officer of the Toronto Scottish serving with the Second Special Air Service Regiment, who accompanied Geoffrey on this survey, describes what happened on one of these excursions.

"Our party consisted of Geoffrey, two sergeants, six men and myself. We left the submarine base, at Malta, in (if I remember correctly) His Majesty's submarine *Unshaken,* under the command of Lieutenant Jack Whitton, R.N.

"After an uneventful trip we arrived off the coast of Mussolini's secret island fortress and for the next twenty-four hours Apple and Jack made a periscope reconnaissance of the fortifications in order to decide on the best place to make a landing.

"At last after an intensive study of both air-photographs and the beach defences, Geoff finally decided on a very high and particularly inaccessible cliff as the best landing place—naturally the success of the operation depended upon taking the enemy by surprise and off their guard—and the harder the climb the greater the surprise.

"The raid had a twofold purpose—to spy out the best landing places for the Allied assault troops and secondly to try and find out the enemy's strength—the latter being very important as our own intelligence did not have much information on the subject.

"In order to gain the necessary information, Geoff had been told to try and capture a sentry and bring him back with us in the hope that he would be able to supply us with the enemy's strength.

"As in all his operations Geoffrey had to have the moon in his favour (that is, to land under the cover of darkness and work in the light of a rising moon). The whole plan was calculated to a split second—so many minutes to get ashore—so many minutes for the raid and so many minutes for the return to the submarine, all this was vitally important otherwise both the submarine and our party might have been discovered in an early dawn.

" During exhaustive tests Apple had decided that R.A.F. rescue dinghies were more suitable than canvas boats and these we blew up as the submarine surfaced half a mile off the coast and launched them over the side.

" Leaving the submarine was a matter of minutes and I soon found myself following Geoff's dinghy ashore—each boat holding five men.

" Our landing was uneventful, and after posting one sentry on the two dinghies Geoff started off in search of the way up that he had already seen from the submarine —no mean feat in the pitch blackness. We had one false start and then began the hardest climb any of us had ever experienced—we pulled ourselves up completely by instinct and every foothold was an insecure one, the rock being volcanic and very porous, crumbling away under our hands and feet.

" By what seemed to be a miracle, Geoff finally got us safely to the top—covered in scratches—for we had decided to wear shorts so that in an emergency swimming would be easier.

" We were nearly discovered as we reached the top of the cliff which was about a hundred feet high at this point. Geoff and the others were crawling away from the edge towards a path that they could dimly see and I was just pulling myself up over the edge when we heard men approaching. We all froze where we were and then to my horror I felt the edge of the cliff on which I was lying begin to crumble.

" The sounds of marching feet and voices were coming much nearer and it became obvious that the Italian patrol was going to pass along the very path by the side of which Geoff was now lying, and there was I slipping slowly back over the edge and not daring to move a muscle for fear of dislodging some of the loose rocks.

" Just as the patrol came level with Geoffrey, who was lying in the gorse not three feet from their feet, the worst happened. A large stone slipped out from beneath me and I waited tensely for the crash as it hit the rocks a hundred feet below me.

" The crash came and Apple and the others prepared to let the patrol have it at short range. But the Italians chattering to each other, apparently didn't hear a sound and passed by, little knowing how near to death they had been. We breathed again and prepared to start the work we had been sent to do.

" Of course, the capturing of a prisoner in our case depended upon silencing him in the quickest way possible, and Apple had decided that the best plan was to crack our particular man on the head with a leaded hosepipe and then lower him down the cliff and away.

" Because of the stiff climb we had encountered, Geoff changed the plan on the spur of the moment—it being impossible to lower or carry an insensible man down the route we had followed. He decided to jump on a sentry, half throttle him and when he had calmed him down, force him to make his own descent.

"Apple therefore detailed me with two men to guard the route down and under no circumstances to give our position away unless directly attacked. He then crept away with the others to find a sentry.

" Hardly had we settled ourselves into our position when the whole guard passed by on their relieving rounds—so close that we could have touched them had we stretched out our hands.

" Geoff and his party also had to lie in the gorse further down the path as the guard passed them and then wait for things to settle down again.

"Very close by they could hear an Italian sentry singing *O sole mio* and decided that he was their man. They crept silently up to him and then Geoff sprang for his throat. In the uncertain light he missed his hold and the sentry let out a scream of fear. Needless to say it was the only sound he made, because by this time four desperate men were sitting all over him and Geoff's fist was literally jammed down his throat—all to no avail—even though Geoff was whispering *Amico! Amico!* in his ear. The Italian reciprocated by getting his teeth well into Geoffrey's wrist.

"The next sentry, about fifty yards away, heard the scream and came running through the gorse towards them. Herstall was nearest to this new danger and although armed only with a rubber truncheon gallantly rushed forward in an attempt to silence him. He was met by a burst of fire in the abdomen, and above the sound of firing I heard him call out to Geoff that he had been hit. That was the last anyone saw or heard of Herstall, because by now the whole guard was aroused and Apple and the other two survivors of his party were deperately fighting them on the cliff edge. Geoff accounted for at least three with his automatic and Sgt. Leigh got one and possibly two.

"By this time things had got so hot that just as my small party had decided to join in the fray Apple shouted "Every man for himself," and as we turned to go back down the cliff I saw him, outlined against the gun flashes and tracer, dive over the edge along with Leigh and the other trooper.

"I thought, as I scrambled madly down the cliff, that I'd seen the last of Apple, but when I reached the bottom he was already there with his two men. How they got down is a mystery because the piece of cliff where they went over was quite strange to them, they were being shot at the whole of the way down, and all the rock was loose and crumbling away. It had taken us nearly three-quarters of an hour to climb the cliff and they got down in about a minute and a half— Sgt. Leigh put his knee out falling part of the way.

" Somehow or other we all managed to find the boats and started to paddle like mad for the rendezvous with *Unshaken* which was lying submerged offshore.

" By this time considerable activity had begun from the shore—Verey lights and machine guns were going off in all directions. Luckily they had no searchlights and we were soon out of Verey light range.

" We had arranged an emergency signal with Jack Whitton just in case of a hurried withdrawal—two grenades to be thrown into the sea, the explosions bringing Whitton to the surface in a hurry.

" Geoff let the grenades off and *Unshaken* broke surface very close by. What a relief it was to see her ! We clambered on board and down the conning tower in double quick time, while hefty sailors slit the rubber boats in little pieces and sank them.

" *Unshaken* immediately submerged and set course for Malta. I'd like to say that the officers and crew couldn't have treated us with more consideration or kindness—they bound up our considerable cuts and bruises and insisted upon giving up their own comfortable bunks to those of us who had been more severely cut.

" One last tribute I want to pay to our naval hosts. Jack's orders had been quite implicit : rather than endanger his submarine he was to abandon us to our fate. But luckily for us he had waited around, although we had been ashore longer than expected, and was prepared to cover our retreat with his 3 inch gun if necessary."

On the return journey the party were to rendezvous with an escort at noon at a position half-way between Pantellaria and Malta. Such was the degree of co-operation afforded by the Admiralty that they arrived by submarine at three minutes to twelve and when they broke surface they were within a couple of minutes' sail of the M.T.B.s waiting there and one minute later the Spitfires from Malta arrived to provide air cover. Geoffrey transferred to motor boat, travelled fast into Malta to a waiting Fortress and was flown straight

back, with Spitfire escort, to the General. The successful outcome of the attack, with the capture of Pantellaria,
is a matter now of history and marked the first stepping
stone towards the conquest of Europe.

Some amusement was caused on their arrival in Malta
when Geoffrey was asked in the mess why his hand
was bandaged. " I've been bitten by a mad Italian,"
was his reply.

Further details of the operation came from a letter
from Captain Bridgman-Evans : " I met Geoffrey and
his patrol in Malta when they arrived back from
Pantellaria. They had been the best part of three
weeks in a submarine. They had been fighting fit when
they started. They looked like death when I saw them.

"About his rendezvous with the M.T.B. and Spitfires
Apple remarked, ' When I climbed through the conning tower there was the M.T.B. not a hundred yards
away and there were the two Spitfires flying overhead.'
The M.T.B. Commander was most disappointed. He
had been told he was picking up the most important
man at the moment in Europe and had expected
Mr. Churchill ! ! "

On 25/6/43 Geoff wrote a letter which led us at
home to hope that things might become a little less
exciting. " Things have been pretty busy here since I
last wrote, but, for a change, I have been very static,
which has been rather pleasant. Actually, I haven't
moved outside the wire round the camp for nearly a
fortnight, except to go on or into the sea. The unit
is now really taking shape and I have considerably more
responsibility than I have had before. In fact, I am
becoming quite a regimental soldier (s'fact, Ian !), as in a
unit of this size the carefree and somewhat haphazard
method of existence of a small irregular unit has to be
very considerably tightened up and adjusted. I still
don't like being regimental, but I suppose it's good for
one, and there is certainly some satisfaction in getting
a smooth running routine going. My own personal
command is now the equivalent of a company. I am
entirely responsible for 'A' Squadron of 12 officers and

156 men, and am also, as Operations Officer, responsible to the Colonel for all the unit's operations—planning, laying on, and executing. And that involves 450 men. Bill Stirling is still in command of the regiment and I think we are building up something that will do great things in the future. You will notice the new address, which should now be used—although I expect Small Scale Raiding Force will still find me for a long time to come. 2nd S.A.S. stands for 2nd Special Air Service Regiment and all ranks are now parachute trained, although that is by no means our only means of entry. I am personally more interested in the other way, as that is where all my own personal experience is. 2nd S.A.S. is, of course, the brother regiment of 1st S.A.S.—David Stirling's force, which did such great work in the Middle East.

" By the way, I forgot to tell you that George Jellicoe is with us with a detachment from 1st S.A.S. and has been here about a month. I greatly admire George—he is one of the very best. His position in 1st S.A.S. is identical with mine. I am also, by the way, the Colonel's deputy and take his operational decisions in his absence."

It was high time Geoffrey had a rest from the ceaseless planning by day and operations by night which had left him little opportunity for sufficient sleep. His tiredness was evident to his brother officers, who entreated him to give himself a rest from operational work. At last he was ordered to do so. He wrote : " By the way, I expect you will be relieved at the following news. I am to do no more operational work personally for at least six months. The reason is that I have been getting a bit ' operationally tired ' lately, although I know it sounds rather unreasonable. I have been getting jumpy, which I am afraid is rather absurd but, under fire, it's a dangerous sign in the leader of a party, even though I am fully able to control myself.

"Although I feel a bit low about planning operations, etc., for other people when I am not going myself, I am quite convinced that some of those who have had less operational work in the past year than I have had, can, for the time being command these small parties in a more vigorous and determined manner than myself at present.

" I suppose also what experience I have gained can be of more value if at the general disposal, and also, of course, as a squadron commander, if that job is to be done properly, I am considerably more tied down. Yes, I am quite resigned to a six months operations rest because I am quite sure that it is the right thing to do.

" But don't worry—I am quite normal—not on the edge of a nervous breakdown or anything, and am actually feeling better every day. I think the state of mind was precipitated by the fact that Roy Bridgman-Evans and I nearly got drowned about two months ago (I didn't tell you before) and it rather shook me. It was a very near thing indeed, but rather a long story. Anyway it has left me with a very healthy respect for surf and big seas, and a complete understanding of how good swimmers can get drowned, which I always scoffed at before. The only satisfaction that I got out of it was the fact that Roy is convinced that if it had not been for me staying with him he would have drowned, although the Lord knows I could do no more than offer him moral support and was in almost as difficult a plight !

" Still, 'nuff said. Otherwise I'm very well, except for a few cuts and sores that will persist in going bad and won't heal up properly. But that is a very normal condition and common to everyone—it must be the climate I think. There is also a lot of a very mild form of dysentery about, nothing serious and only spasmodic. Sun is now normal all day, very little cloud and only very, very occasional rain, heavy thunder storms. Nights are still in general quite cool and very pleasant."

His letter of 27th June, 1943, read : " I found Malta very interesting in small doses, but I should hate to be there long—it's terribly dry and stony—stone walks, stone houses, and stony ground everywhere—and there are no trees nor green vegetation anywhere on the island. Now that the episodes are finished, I suppose there is no harm in telling you that Pantalleria and Lampedusa were the main reasons for my Malta visits. You probably saw accounts in the press of a raid on 'Lampy' that we did—it was from enemy communiqué sources and it was interesting to note their exaggerations, both as regards numbers involved and casualties, on both sides. Our small party was reported as 'five companies of Commandos'! Actually 'Pants' was the place that interested me and where most of my time was spent. Quite an exciting little place with its 13,000 troops in a few square miles, so it was an interesting test of our small party technique. I spent a lot of time in the very close vicinity of the place, two or three weeks in total I should think, and now feel to know the appearance of every rock and stone and house and headland on it in detail. Strange to look back to the only time I had previously seen the place—as blue volcanic looking peaks on the horizon on one of our summer cruises, remember? By the way, I have seen Etna again—from 120 miles away with the evening light shining on the snow cap.

"How pleasant my room at home must look after its repainting, etc. Maybe I shall be seeing it again before long—lovely! Did I tell you there is every prospect (say 75 per cent. chance) of my returning home about August? I won't be sorry to come back in a couple of months' time but I feel there are many people who deserve a trip home more."

On 6/7/43 he wrote from No. 2 Special Air Service Regiment, B.N.A.F. : "Have just been away from camp for four days on a longish circuit. I saw Tunis, but was not impressed. Also Carthage in passing. Then down to Sousse, the most bombed place I have ever seen (not a single habitable house in the main part of the town) and also Hammamet and Monastir, a fascinating place (on the coast just south of Sousse, like Salé (near Rabat, remember?) and very attractive looking and Arabesque—until you smelt it!—on a rather lovely bit of coast too.   Also saw some astonishing mirages on the mud flats south of Sousse.   You would swear you were looking at pools and lakes, etc. ! The road, Tunis-Sousse, is fascinating with its evidences of the campaign there—littered with burnt-out and blown up wrecks of tanks, vehicles, guns, etc., posted all over with mines and booby trap warnings, ' clear lanes,' etc.   Anti-tank   ditches,   wire,   pill-boxes   (mostly ' knocked-out ') are much in evidence in certain places, especially Enfidaville, as also are German, Italian and British graves—just in twos and threes with rough wooden crosses everywhere. All the German ones have the soldier's tin hat on them always. Interesting to see the war booty—immense quantities—a lot of which is now in our use, and one sees whole convoys of German lorries with German drivers too ! Prisoners for labour duties are seen everywhere and appear to be happy, especially the Italians.   We have fifty permanently in the camp here and they need no guarding. They wait, cook, etc., as well as doing heavier labour work, and seem to really enjoy being out of the war with a job to do ! I go away from the camp again tomorrow, perhaps for two or three weeks, but should get mail forwarded at intervals. Dearest love. God bless.   Geoffrey.''

That was his last letter home.   The object of the tour he described was to arrange for an airborne expedition in which about a dozen of his paratroop commandos were to be dropped by parachute in Sicily north of Randazzo, which is north of Etna, and there capture and hold an important strategic bridge in advance of the Allied landing in Sicily and ease the way for this to be accomplished.   His brother officers say that it was arranged that although Geoffrey, as responsible for operations in No. 2 Special Air Service Regiment in North Africa should plan the flight and the landing, he himself could not be spared from duties in Africa and therefore must not make the drop into Sicily.

Geoffrey went off to Kairouan—the rock-dwelling village—from the aerodrome of which it was arranged the flight to Sicily should start. On the night of the 12th July, 1943, Geoffrey telephoned H.Q. asking permission for the flight that night as the conditions were perfect, and the General acquiesced. Later a despatch rider arrived from Geoffrey stating that he had decided to go on the flight himself in order to be sure of the best landing place for the parachute commandos and with a view to determining definitely the spot to which reinforcements should be sent the following night, and stating that he expected to be back about 1 a.m. on the 13th.

Five days later, there arrived the saddest tidings that ever reached his family. It was a letter from his friend and brother officer, Major Ian Collins. It read :—

" I am afraid I have some very bad news for you. Geoffrey is missing. I still hope we may have some news and if so I will send a cable to C.O.H.Q. and they will send it straight on to you.

" You will realise how I feel for all of you as Geoffrey and I have worked so closely together for over a year and he was a great friend to have. I will give you all the particulars I can. Geoffrey was in charge of an operation, though not actually due to land himself. He went out in the aircraft on 12th July with a party who were to land by parachute in order that he could help to despatch them and have a good look at the country for future reference. The pilot was a Wing Commander and one of our ablest men. We have had no news of the aircraft since it left. There are thus the following possibilities :—

(1) It may have been shot down, or engine may have failed, over the sea getting there, and this is I fear most likely.

(2) It may have been shot down by enemy night fighter or flak, though as far as we know there was little chance of this happening, as there was little in the area.

In either of above cases, aircraft might have only been damaged and the passengers, all of whom wore parachutes, may have been able to jump out, so they may have landed in Sicily and be prisoners or behind the enemy lines and free and safe, and in either case we would not have news for some time.

(3) Aircraft may have dropped the parachute party and crashed on way back through engine failure, and if so Geoffrey might have jumped and be somewhere in Sicily.

(4) Aircraft might have flown into a hill. It was hilly country but it was a very clear night and pilot was experienced.

" I think you would rather I gave you all the facts, which I have done. You will see there is still real reason for hoping Geoffrey may be all right, and every effort will be made to find out. You will almost certainly receive a cable from War Office in due course to say he is missing ; but I will be the first almost to hear any news and will see a message is sent you immediately I have any news at all.

" Words cannot adequately express our feelings at a time like this, and Geoffrey is irreplaceable to so many of us : he has done great work out here and I have seen a lot of him and was with him for three days at the beginning of this month and again for a night on the 9th July. He was so well and cheery and confident, and I spoke to him on the telephone on the 12th just before he left.

" I am afraid this is a very difficult letter to write and I have only a very short time to write it and get it home to you quickly. Some of the facts are at present secret, as you will realise, so please keep them to yourself in case it prejudices Geoffrey's return, if he is still behind the enemy lines.

"All my sympathy is with you and your family in the anxious period of waiting for news and I only pray I may be able to send you some good news shortly."

A later letter showed that two aircraft made the journey on Monday night, the 12th July. "Geoffrey was on board the first, which was an Albemarle number PMP.1446, piloted by Wing Commander May, one of the most experienced officers on the coast. The aircraft left Kairouan at 8 p.m. and as the flight was $2\frac{1}{2}$ hours, would be expected back soon after 1 a.m. The second aircraft followed the first ten minutes after. Their course lay entirely over the sea until a few miles south of Taormina, when they turned abruptly inland to Randazzo and discharged the ten or eleven men, all of whom have since been accounted for and all of whom except one safely reached the American Army operating along the North coast of Sicily a few days ago. These men definitely state that the Albemarle with Geoffrey was seen by them leaving Randazzo. This is a hilly country, but the night was brilliantly clear, which was the reason why Geoffrey asked permission to go that night. The pilot was very experienced and the Air Force do not think it probable that they could have run into a hillside.

" The route back was scheduled direct from Randazzo to a few miles south of Taormina, and out to sea and back over the same route on which they had gone out. The second aircraft discharged its men and reported back safely and had not seen the first aeroplane, although they were flying on the same route ; but this is not surprising at night.

" There was very little enemy flak in the Randazzo area and very few enemy aircraft about."

The difficulty of obtaining any information about the aircraft, or what had happened, was complicated by the activity which followed two or three days later when the full battle for Sicily was in progress and there was much movement of aircraft and ships. Major Collins made arrangements to be informed by Air Force, Admiralty or Army of whatever evidence came to light in regard to the aircraft, the Wing Commander, or Geoffrey, but none ever transpired.

A later letter from Major Collins dated 27/7/43 read :
" I am afraid I have no more news at all that I can give
you of Geoffrey. We have made exhaustive enquiries
but there is no indication at all as to what might have
happened. I am, of course, still trying to find out more,
and if he should have had to make a forced landing it is
unlikely that we would have had any news yet. We only
know now that the party he went out with were landed
safely, so something must have happened on the way back."

Again Major Collins wrote on the 31st July, 1943 :
" I am afraid there is still no news at all, and it is
practically certain that the only news we would get
now would be if aircraft had to make a forced landing
and Geoffrey was a prisoner of war or still wandering
about undetected. I was away all day to-day to see the
R.A.F. concerned and spoke to a pilot who had gone
out with him that night before they separated and went
their different ways. They all spoke so highly of the
Wing Commander who was flying the plane Geoffrey
was in, and I know from what everyone tells me what
an exceptionally fine person and pilot he was. I think
every possible angle has been approached to try and
get news, though you will realise how difficult it is to
get detailed news of one aircraft when there are so
many about on a night when a big battle is on.

" I am so sorry I cannot help at all with news, and
I do feel for you all so much. As I said in my first
letter, one must go on hoping. I can only tell you again
how well Geoffrey had done out here and how much
his work had been appreciated. He was very happy,
and as full of enthusiasm and vitality as ever. War is
so destructive and it always seems to take away the best,
but I always feel it is so much harder for those who
are left behind (his family) as the 'best' are the type who
so willingly give their all and no sacrifice is great enough
for them. They live happily so death has no fear for
them. You must all feel so proud of all Geoffrey has done.

" I only hope still that some good news will come
but I am afraid I am not very hopeful. I feel it very
much myself as Geoffrey and I have shared so much

M

in the last fifteen months. He was a great friend in every way. All my sympathy."

Once again we heard from Major Collins, on 12/8/43 : " I have just arrived back and will try and telephone you to-day. I am afraid I have no more news at all of Geoffrey that I can give you. I am so sorry. All possible sources have been informed so that if any news comes through I should hear at once. I was over in Sicily and made all enquiries there. His aircraft was in the area north of Randazzo when last seen and was due to come back between Taormina and Catania and then due south, and the hope is that it may have been forced down and that he is a prisoner. All my sympathy in this anxious period."

Notification was received from the War Office as follows :—

War Office.

30th August, 1943.

I am directed to inform you that the notification that your son, Major J. G. Appleyard, D.S.O., M.C. and Bar, Royal Army Service Corps, was reported missing on the 12th/13th July, 1943, in North Africa, has been received at the War Office with regret.

No further information is available at present, but all possible enquiries are being made and any further information received by this Department will be sent to you immediately.

Despite continuous enquiries and searching by land and sea no evidence was found which could contribute information as to the aircraft's disappearance, and after the fullest possible investigation the following letter was finally received :—

War Office.

4th March, 1944.

With reference to War Office letter of the 30th August, 1943, I am directed to inform you that your son, Major J. G. Appleyard, D.S.O., M.C. and Bar, Royal Army Service Corps, was in charge of a special operation on the night of the 12th/13th July, 1943, and was travelling in an aircraft for observational purposes. The aircraft did not return from the operation and nothing has been seen or heard of it or the passengers since.

In all the circumstances the conclusion has been reached, with deep regret, that your son lost his life, and it is consequently being officially recorded that Major J. G. Appleyard, D.S.O., M.C. and Bar, Royal Army Service Corps, is presumed to have been killed in action on the 13th July, 1943.

I am to convey to you an expression of the sincere sympathy of the Army Council.

This official notification was followed by the warmhearted letter sent to relatives by H.M. The King :—

Buckingham Palace.

The Queen and I offer you our heartfelt sympathy in your great sorrow.

We pray that your country's gratitude for a life so nobly given in its service may bring you some measure of consolation.

GEORGE R.I.

It is a tragic coincidence that the date Geoffrey is officially presumed to have been killed, July 13th, 1943, is the very same day as that on which Graham Hayes, his boyhood friend and close companion in so many Commando raids and undertakings, was shot by the Germans in Paris, as previously described. It is the belief of both their families that their close and intimate comradeship still endures.

This narrative has quoted letters from Captain Roy Bridgman-Evans, M.C., and it is fitting that some reference should be made to his own remarkable story. He was in command of the parachute party in the plane which followed ten minutes behind Geoffrey's in the early morning of July 13th. Roy's plane had to run the gauntlet of intense Ack-Ack fire, the bursts of which were throwing the plane about so badly that the electrical system became faulty. When the pilot began to open the bomb doors, preparatory to dropping the containers containing the food and ammunition for the parachutists, the light in the fuselage which was used to give them a visual signal of when to jump, accidentally flashed on. Roy and his party immediately baled out and had a very rough passage to earth, because the pilot, not knowing that the light had gone on, had not slowed down and the plane was still doing over 200 miles an hour. Also, because their departure from the plane was not noticed by the pilot for some minutes, the containers with most of their equipment were not dropped with them, and they found themselves on the ground miles from their intended dropping zone armed only with pistols. Some German troops actually saw them come down and they were all captured when daylight came.

After a few days they were sent over to Southern Italy and one evening found themselves on a railway station waiting for a train to take them north to a prison camp. Roy decided to attempt an escape and got some of his men to talk to the sentries and keep them occupied. Then with three others he climbed a wall at the end of the platform and managed to get clean away. That night they had to cross a very wide river and a railway viaduct seemed the only way over. They had started to cross when they were challenged by a German sentry. Luckily one of Roy's little party spoke fluent German and called out that everything was all right and that they were a party of German soldiers who had been ordered to cross the bridge. It was very dark and the sentry let them through, although in so doing each one, clad in British uniform, passed right in front of him! The party finally reached the coast, stole a boat but were only just clear of the shore when a sentry saw them and opened fire. Two of the men were wounded and all were recaptured.

Roy was moved to an officers' prison camp north of Naples. There he organised the digging of an escape tunnel and had completed twenty-two yards of it when orders came for all prisoners to be moved to a camp at Bologna further north. It was heartbreaking to be moved because the tunnel was only two days from completion.

After ten days at the camp at Bologna the Italians capitulated and the Germans took over. Roy eventually found himself in the officers' prison camp at Fort Bismarck near Strasbourg. After a careful examination of the barbed wire he discovered that there was one place alongside the main guardroom which could not be seen by any of the guards when the sentry, watching that part of the perimeter, was at the end of his beat. In broad daylight and with everything timed to a split second, Roy and another officer cut the wire, slipped through and lay low in a tiny patch of scrub growing just outside the wire. Not daring to move they remained here for two hours whilst every few minutes a sentry passed within five feet of them.

When darkness fell they crawled away undetected and walking only at night and lying up in the woods by day, covered two hundred miles over the Vosges Mountains in a little over a week.

Once over the frontier they managed to contact the "underground" movement who fitted them out with civilian clothes, forged identity papers and money. Thus equipped they travelled openly by rail to Paris where they separated. Roy spent one day in the French capital, and then caught the night train for Bordeaux. He even had the incredible audacity and courage to have dinner on the train at a table next to one at which four German officers were sitting.

He crossed the Pyrenees into Spain with a local guide and without declaring his nationality to the Spanish, went by rail to Barcelona. Here he managed to get safely into the British Consulate, past the patrolling Spanish sentries who were posted in an attempt to prevent escaped British prisoners of war from gaining the protection of their Consulate. Under the protection of the British Consul he was conveyed from Barcelona to Madrid and then on to Gibraltar whence he was flown home.

From the time of his escape at Strasbourg to the time he set foot in England was only thirty-seven days ! —truly a magnificent achievement for which he was awarded the Military Cross.

In July 1945, Lt.-Col. Ian Collins wrote : "I have intended to write to you for some time to tell you how successful the S.A.S. has been in operations in North-West Europe. We got the S.A.S. going on a really big scale but a lot of its success is due to the pioneer work done in the early stages by people like Gus, Apple and others, and it is so sad that they have not lived to see the successful growth of their work and how their ideas and ideals have been carried on."

Even after the apparently final official communication, Geoffrey's family still hoped that somehow he might have escaped from the aircraft before it crashed and might be a prisoner in Northern Italy or Germany, and resolved not to give up hope until the end of the European struggle brought the return of the last prisoner of war.

But though good news came to many families it passed by Geoff's.

It was hard to realise that after so many hairbreadth escapes on land and sea, in submarines and in aircraft, Geoffrey had fallen at last and joined Gus and Graham and the great host of those who fought and died that England might live.

The passage of time fails to ease the pain of his loss, but it likewise fails to dim the rich, happy memories of his radiant young life.

Although he may not come back he never seems far away. Often indeed he seems very near ; not least so when we are tramping over his beloved Yorkshire fells, the wind carrying the varied sounds of the moorland— the splash of a nearby stream, the whisper of the long grass, the bleating of lambs and suddenly, the lovely, bubbling cry of a curlew—the bird he loved above all others. Then we recall what Geoffrey said one day as the same call came faintly across the moor : " That's how I'd like to return to earth when my time comes." How like Geoff that his wish should be so simple ! But the curlew to him typified the very spirit of the wide rolling fells and—*Freedom*.

But we believe he fulfils a bigger part—that his spirit still lives on and fights for the establishment of the new world for which he gave his life.

Moreover, we know, that though it may be long before we all meet again, when we do, it will be like one of those home-comings on leave, when in the joy of reunion we forgot we had ever been apart.

* *Because of you we will be glad and gay,*
Remembering you, we will be brave and strong ;
And hail the advent of each dangerous day,
And meet the last adventure with a song.

And, as you proudly gave your jewelled gift,
We'll give our lesser offering with a smile,
Nor falter on that path where, all too swift,
You led the way and leapt the golden stile.

Whether new paths, new heights to climb, you find,
Or gallop through the unfooted asphodel,
We know you know we shall not lag behind,

Nor halt to waste a moment on a fear ;
And you will speed us onward with a cheer,
And wave beyond the stars that all is well.

MAURICE BARING

Quoted by the kind permission of the late Major the Hon. Maurice Baring who wrote this poem after his friend, Julian Grenfell, D.S.O., was killed in the Great War of 1914-18.

CHAPTER VII

AS OTHERS KNEW HIM

The following extracts are quoted from the vast number of tributes received from friends made by Geoffrey at each stage of his career :—

SCHOOL DAYS

FROM HIS HOUSEMASTER (L.G.) :

" I should like to pay a very sincere tribute to Geoffrey, a tribute of gratitude. I think of him as one of the most upright, sincere, courageous and kindly boys that I've had the privilege of teaching, and as a friend whose influence was invariably for good. I'm sure that such qualities as he possessed are lasting ones : his life was rooted in the things that endure, and his personality, I'm convinced, cannot have been overcome by death of the body."

FROM HIS CLASSICS MASTER (B.S.) :

" We remember, as though it were yesterday, Geoffrey as a charming, considerate, very kindly boy coming to tea with us at Penn House in his first days at Bootham—the beginning of a friendship with him renewed again and again as he visited the school and greeted us with his friendly, honest handshake and the expression on his handsome face that radiated joy and delight making one feel instantly the warmth of his generous heart. Geoffrey was one of the best boys we have ever had at Bootham. He combined the great qualities of mind and character so well, but was so humble in his spirit whatever his achievements and success.

" I do not doubt that you were proud of him, but you would have been still more proud had you been able to see (just what a parent never can see, save through another's eyes), the way in which he turned every circumstance to some good end, every moment of time to some promising effort, using his great gifts not only on things near at hand but with a growing vision of far horizons.

" Geoffrey was one of those rare boys who make a school-master a better man than he would have been if he had never known him. And the same truth is plain to see in the soldierly obituary notice in *The Times* : he made men into good men by his very association with them, by his unflinching purpose, his courage, his radiant disposition—the whole man of him a living inspiration."

UNIVERSITY DAYS

FROM HIS CLOSEST COLLEGE FRIEND—AN AUSTRALIAN (W.R.) :

" Geoff was quite honestly the finest man I know. Though I didn't realise it till later I know that a large part of my fondness for Geoff was simply hero worship ; anything he did he did well.

" Knowing Geoff so well, his wonderful war record hardly surprised me, it's just what I'd have expected of him. I can imagine just how much his men would worship him ; he was a born leader and from my knowledge of the Army I know he's the sort of man that men will follow anywhere ; it's leaders like Geoff who make the British Army so good ; that's just plain fact."

SKI-ING

FROM A U.S.A. FELLOW RACER (D.B.) :

" Geoff was an outstanding fellow : I only knew him for the short month we were together in Norway at Easter, 1939, but since that trip I had always regarded him as the outstanding Englishman I knew, and, what is infinitely more important, one of the warmest friends I had.

" There were many things on that trip which set Geoff apart from the rest of the group, and which naturally drew us together. First, perhaps, he skied for the love of it, for the freedom of the mountains and the zest of the race, and less for the renown or the social aspects of it. He had the spirit of a mountain goat. Many a time we took side trips, leaving our more contented members below, to climb the highest peak in striking range. Some of us have an inexplicable yearning to get to the highest peak, to have a look at the world, beautiful and solitary and primitive, from a special viewpoint.

"Another thing we had in common was the feeling that the comradeship of skiers is invariably one of unusually fine fellows. Among them race and nationality are more or less discarded, except for those whose capacity to appreciate good fellowship has been perverted by false, nationalistic doctrines. Geoff was always the heartiest of companions, and admired and liked by everyone who knew him.

" Your sense of loss is shared by people all over the world, in Switzerland, Norway, France, Canada, America—just to name a few countries. And they share, too, your pride in his courage, his devotion to your way of life, his zest for life. Tagore once wrote : ' The world is richer for the love that has been lost in it.' Had he thought about it he might have added that the world is stronger for the lives that have been lost in it."

WORKS COLLEAGUES

F.L. : " I saw very early, when first the fury of war caught us, that in his heart Geoffrey ' vowed devotion to the rights of men : ' deliberately seeking the hard and dangerous way, keen and eager to be used, to give just all his rich qualities ' for all the lovely things worth fighting for.' We all love him for it and for the grand and gallant boy he is. For me personally—may I say this —he is and will always be the very embodiment of strong, alert and vigorous manhood, of courage and ' right direction.' To-day I have talked to many of his friends at the factory. There is deep sadness everywhere."

H.W. : " Everyone who knew Geoffrey knew the great promise his life held for the future and his loss is shared and mourned in a wide circle outside his own home.

" I have been throwing memory back over the past years and in particular to the time—after his return from Dunkirk—when he reached the decision to volunteer for the perilous job of the Commandos.

" Geoffrey had a clear vision of what had to be achieved in this war before the foundations of the future could be laid and he chose—as he would do—one of the most dangerous and exacting tasks. He brought to his new work all the energy, leadership and above all the friendliness which endeared him to all under his command and to all his friends.

"His work brought him into contact with many other grand fellows of character and right outlook and the tragedy is that the war is claiming so many of those the world can least afford to lose."

BUSINESS

A.D. : " He was a verray parfit gentil knyght."

ARMY

The Lord Louis Mountbatten, g.c.v.o., d.s.o., a.d.c., Supreme Allied Commander, South East Asia. (Formerly, Chief of Combined Operations) :

"He was a grand leader and I was proud to have him in my command."

R.H.B.-E. (Geoff's next in command in North Africa) :

"If ever one man loved another, I loved Geoffrey. I often think of him even now. I am proud that I had the honour to serve under such a very fine man and friend."

F.V. : "A business friend told me the other day that he was. staying some time ago at Morecambe and met a couple of men who were on special training. They happened to speak of Leeds and he asked casually if they knew Geoff. One of them spoke up at once : ' Yes, of course I do. He's my officer, the best fellow who ever walked. I'd go anywhere with him.' "

J.G. (a fellow officer) :

" I saw and worked with Geoff a great deal for more than six months and during that time I formed a great attachment for him. In some ways he represented just about my ideal of Christian, chivalrous and courageous manhood coupled with a great spirit of adventure and charm."

J.H.S. (GEOFFREY'S BATMAN) :

"He was not an Army Officer to me, but a great friend."

J.D. (A FELLOW OFFICER) :

"Immediately I met him in West Africa I was captivated by the blend in him of extreme courage and great gentleness, a combination of qualities in these latter days so rare that it lacks a name but which once was known as chivalry and the embodiment of the highest English tradition."

I.K.W. (A FELLOW COMMANDO) :

"Everyone who had the honour and privilege to serve with him was immediately under the spell of his personality. We are all better men thanks to Geoffrey. Just before I jumped into Burma last year I got an attack of the 'jitters' as the aircraft approached our dropping zone. Then a thought flashed through my mind : 'What is death ? If I die I meet Gus, Apple and Graham,' and from that moment I was calm and contented. I have often wondered if they inspired that thought."

D.W. (GUS'S SISTER) :

"I know of nobody who was so warmly liked, trusted and admired as Apple was by everyone—from officers of the highest rank, as you know, down to the charwoman who looks after us here. Whenever he came to stay either here or at Lowndes Square everyone immediately brightened up—the atmosphere seemed different. A spirit like Apple's never really dies and he will never, never be forgotten by his friends. Both he and Gus to me are the real spirit of England."

A.H. (A FELLOW OFFICER) :

"Geoffrey ! his name of course is also 'Galahad.' To my mind Apple was the very heart and soul of honour and I have what I can only call a 'Generous Envy' when I think of Gus and Apple and the others together now. I don't think the banner of England has ever been more proudly borne. They set a great problem for survivors ! "

I.G.C. (A FELLOW OFFICER WHO WROTE THIS TRIBUTE FOR " THE
    TIMES ") :

" It is hard to realise that 'Apple' is gone and his loss to his
family, to his friends and to his unit is irreplaceable.   Behind a
calm, quiet manner lay an outstanding ability.   He had great powers
of leadership and the determination to see a job through.   There
would be no fuss, but any job allotted to him would be studied
and planned in great detail so that nothing should be left to
chance.

" Few have had the same responsibility placed on them at so
young an age and his work brought him into close contact with
senior officers of all services.

" With such ability and personality he soon became a first-
class navigator and was allotted the rare distinction, as a military
officer, of being placed in command of naval craft on raiding
operations.   He was equally fitted to operate on sea, on land
or from the air.

" The full history of his exploits cannot yet be written, but
apart from operations he had done great work in training and
building up the special unit of which he was second in command
when he was killed.

" Men like 'Apple' do not fear death, their conscience is
clear, but their loss is felt all the more by those who are left
behind.   He would surely have done great work in the task that
lies in front of us after the war and helped to lead the country,
as he led his men, to realise the good and lovely things which
make life worth living.

" England has lost an officer of exceptional ability and courage,
but his work will live on and all who have served with him will
be grateful for the inspiration he has given them."

HOME FRIENDS

E.W. : " What lovely memories you have !   For you couldn't
have had a finer son.   He was so splendid at everything he
undertook.   You must feel very proud of all the honours he
won, both military and others.   But you must feel thankful
most of all that he was so greatly loved, and so utterly good,
and not afraid to show his colours.   I think he must have helped
a great many by his courage."

P.C.S. : " Here was a man with an achievement in the arts of peace quite brilliant, and with a safe prospect of a life full of enjoyment (for few could live a fuller life in the best sense than he did before the war)—a man who might, more than most, have clung to his home blessings, and yet he joined the R.A.S.C. before war broke out, threw himself into the worst hazards again and again, and a life that was the biggest contrast to what he had experienced that one could imagine. And the end almost a certainty !

" We are apt to think ' what a waste of excellence !' But we *must* be wrong to think in terms of years and age."

E.M. : " He is not merely a wonderful memory, but a legendary figure. His capacity for work, for pleasure, his joy, his quick sympathy would have made him an outstanding figure in any generation."

J.H.H. (AN APPRECIATION WHICH APPEARED IN THE LOCAL PRESS) :

"As one who has known Geoffrey Appleyard since boyhood days, and watched his development with deep interest, I write these few words of appreciation.

" Geoffrey was one of the choicest characters it has been my lot to meet on my journey through life ; it was always a delight to be in his company. An intense nature lover, a fine sportsman and a great gentleman, there was nothing mean or tawdry in his make-up. Despite his many triumphs in athletics, he was the most modest of men. Had he been spared, he would undoubtedly have had a great future. He was a born leader, and men would follow him through thick and thin. He has gone on ahead, and our County and Country are the poorer as a result, but his life has been an inspiration, and his memory a benediction.

"A year ago he was offered a comparatively safe administrative post, but this he refused never counting the cost, sufficient for him was the plain path of duty, which he followed unhesitatingly and unswervingly.

" To those who mourn his loss we pray our Heavenly Father may assuage the anguish of bereavement, and leave only the cherished memory of the loved, and solemn pride in having laid the costliest of all sacrifices on the altar of freedom."

Rev. LESLIE D. WEATHERHEAD, M.A. (Minister of the
City Temple, London) :

" I knew Geoffrey from his schooldays onwards. At the time
of his early manhood I said to a friend, ' If a visitor dropped down
from Mars and visited each country to find out what earth's
inhabitants were like, and if I had the chance to suggest whom
such a visitor should meet in England, I should suggest Geoffrey
Appleyard.' His love of adventure, his sense of humour, his self-
forgetfulness, his chivalry, his love of birds and poetry, and his
unobtrusive, but real, religion were all woven into the texture
of a character as strong and beautiful as any I have ever known.
Perhaps all can be summed up by saying that he revelled in
life—physically, mentally and spiritually, and made all with
whom he came into contact feel that life was a good thing as he
lived it.

" Nothing could persuade me that this gay troubadour is dead.
His body he may have given for England, but his soul lives on,
part of the wealth of the universe, for it possessed qualities that
do not die and over which war has no power."

Any further information or details of the matter published in
this book concerning Geoffrey's activities in North Africa and
Sicily in 1943 would be gratefully received by J. E. Appleyard,
The Manor House, Linton, Wetherby, Yorkshire.